Japanese Monograph No. 71

ARMY OPERATIONS IN CHINA

December 1941–December 1943

PREPARED BY
HEADQUARTERS, USAFFE
AND EIGHTH U.S. ARMY (REAR)

DISTRIBUTED BY
OFFICE OF THE CHIEF OF MILITARY HISTORY
DEPARTMENT OF THE ARMY

Published by Books Express Publishing
Copyright © Books Express, 2011
ISBN 978-1-78039-501-2

Books Express publications are available from all good retail and online booksellers. For publishing proposals and direct ordering please contact us at: info@books-express.com

PREFACE

This monograph is one of a series prepared under instructions from the Supreme Commander for the Allied Powers to the Japanese Government (SCAPIN No. 126, 12 Oct 1945). The series covers not only the operations of the Japanese armed forces during World War II, but also their operations in China and Manchuria which preceded the world conflict. The studies were written by former officers of the Japanese Army and Navy under the supervision of the Historical Records Section of the First (Army) and Second (Navy) Demobilization Bureaus of the Japanese Government. Original manuscripts were translated by U.S. Army translation service. Extensive editing was accomplished by the Japanese Research Division of the Office of the Military History Officer, Headquarters, United States Army Forces, Far East and Eighth United States Army (Rear).

This monograph describes military operations in the China Theater from the time of the outbreak of the Pacific war until the end of 1943. Under the direction of the Reports and Statistical Section of the Demobilization Bureau, the basic manuscript was written by former Lt Col Heizo Ishiwari, a former member of the War History Section of the Army General Staff, assisted by the following former officers: Colonel Seitaro Takei and Major Sentaro Azuma of the 11th Army, Lt Cols Hideo Ono and Kenji Shindo of the 13th Army and Colonel Chiyoshi Shimoda of the 23d Army from official telegrams, notes and personal recollections. It was necessary for the Japanese Research Division to conduct extensive research in order to evaluate the information, to check both facts and dates and to add pertinent data. In addition, as the manuscript was submitted with very inadequate maps, this office prepared the many maps required to illustrate the text. Spelling of place names in this monograph is that used in AMS 5301.

The editor received valuable assistance in research and in the preparation of maps from Tadao Shudo, formerly a lieutenant colonel on the staff of the 11th Army in central China and later a member of the Army General Staff and Air Army General Staff.

Other monographs covering the operations of the Japanese armed forces in the China area are:

Mono No	Title	Period
70*	China Area Operations Record	Jul 37 - Nov 41
72	Army Operations in China	Jan 44 - Aug 45
74*	Operations in the Kun-lun-kuan Area	Dec 39 - Feb 40
76	Air Operations in the China Area	Jul 37 - Aug 45
129*	China Area Operations Record: Command of China Expeditionary Army	Aug 43 - Aug 45
130*	China Area Operations Record: Sixth Area Army Operations	May 44 - Aug 45
166	China Incident Naval Air Operations	Jul 37 - Nov 37
178*	North China Area Operations Record	Jul 37 - May 41
179*	Central China Area Operations Record	1937 - 1941
180*	South China Area Operations Record	1937 - 1941

* Indicates edit completed.

Tokyo, Japan
31 May 1956

Table of Contents

	Page
CHAPTER 1 – Operations in Chinese Theater After the Outbreak of the Pacific War	15
Situation in China After the Outbreak of the Pacific War	16
Maintenance of Strength in China	18
Hong Kong Operation	21
General Situation Prior to the Operation	21
Operational Command	27
Concentration of Japanese Forces	38
Progress of Operation	38
Movement of Chinese Forces During the Hong Kong Operation	48
Administration	48
CHAPTER 2 – 2d Changsha Operation	53
Situation Prior to the Operation	53
Progress of Operation	58
Reverse Turn After 2d Changsha Operation	66
Progress of Battle in the Eastern District of the 9th War Sector	72
Battle in the Northern Area of the Yangtze River	73
CHAPTER 3 – Chekiang-Kiangsi Operation	79

	Page
General Situation Prior to the Operation	79
Operational Command	85
Preparations for the Operation	89
Progress of 13th Army's Operation	91
Progress of 11th Army's Operation	99
Temporary Occupation of Tracts along the Chekiang-Kiangsi Railway	105
Garrisoning and Offensive Operations by the 13th Army	106
Yungchia Operation	109
Sungyang Operation	110
11th Army's Operation in the Chekiang-Kiangsi Area	111
Reverse Operation	116
Reverse Movement of the 13th Army	117
Reverse Movement of the 11th Army	121
Casualties During Reverse Operations	121
Plan to Capture Szechwan Province	121
Transfer and Reorganization of China Expeditionary Army Forces	125
CHAPTER 4 - Operations in 1943	129
Luichow Peninsula Operation and the Occupation of Kuangchou Wan	129
Progress of Operation	130

	Page
Kuangte Operation	134
Operation North of the Yangtze River	138
Operational Command	142
Progress of Operation	143
Operation South of the Yangtze River	148
Situation Prior to the Operation	148
Progress of Operation	149
Withdrawal	155
Changte Operation	157
Situation Prior to the Operation	157
Progress of Operation	164

CHARTS

		Page
No 1	Standard Table of Strength Assigned to the Capture of Hong Kong	29
No 2	An Outline of the Tactical Organization of Forces of the 23d Army for the Hong Kong Operation	32
No 3	Disposition of Troops for Invasion of Hong Kong	46

MAPS

No 1	Disposition of both friendly and enemy forces prior to the Hong Kong Operation, end Nov 1941	23

		Page
No 2	Disposition of 23d Army in South China end Nov 1941	25
No 3	Concentration of 23d Army for Hong Kong Operation, 1-6 Dec 1941	39
No 4	Progress of the Hong Kong Operation, 8-25 Dec 1941	43
No 5	General Situation before the Second Changsha Operation, early Dec 1941	55
No 6	Second Changsha Operation, 24 Dec 1941 - 6 Jan 1942	59
No 7	The Reverse Turn After Second Changsha Operation, 4-15 Jan 1942	67
No 8	General Situation in Central China 13th Army Zone, mid-May 1942	81
No 9	General Situation in Central China 11th Army Zone, mid-May 1942	83
No 10	Progress of the 13th Army in the Chekiang-Kiangsi Operation, 15 May - 1 Jul 1942	93
No 11	Progress of 11th Army in Chekiang-Kiangsi Operation, 31 May - 1 Jul 1942	101
No 12	13th Army Disposition and Yungchia and Sungyang Operations, 20 Jun - 3 Aug 1942	107
No 13	The 11th Army's Operation in the Chekiang-Kiangsi Area, 15 Jun - 6 Jul 1942	113
No 14	The Reverse Movement of the 13th Army and Occupation of the Newly Captured Area, 15 Aug - Mid-Sep 1942	119
No 15	Luichow Peninsula Operation and Occupation of Kuangchou Wan, 16 - 20 Feb 1943	131
No 16	Kuangte Operation, 30 Sep - 10 Oct 1943	135

		Page
No 17	General Situation before the Operation North of the Yangtze River, Jan 1943	139
No 18	Operation North of the Yangtze River 15 Feb - end Mar 1943	145
No 19	Operation South of the Yangtze River 5 - 29 May 1943	151
No 20	General Situation of Enemy and Friendly Forces in Wuchang-Hankou Area, end Oct 1943	159
No 21	Changte Operation, 2 Nov - 4 Dec 1943	167

General Reference Maps

Chapter 1	12-13
Chapter 2	52
Chapter 3	78
Chapter 4	128
Index	171

CHAPTER 1

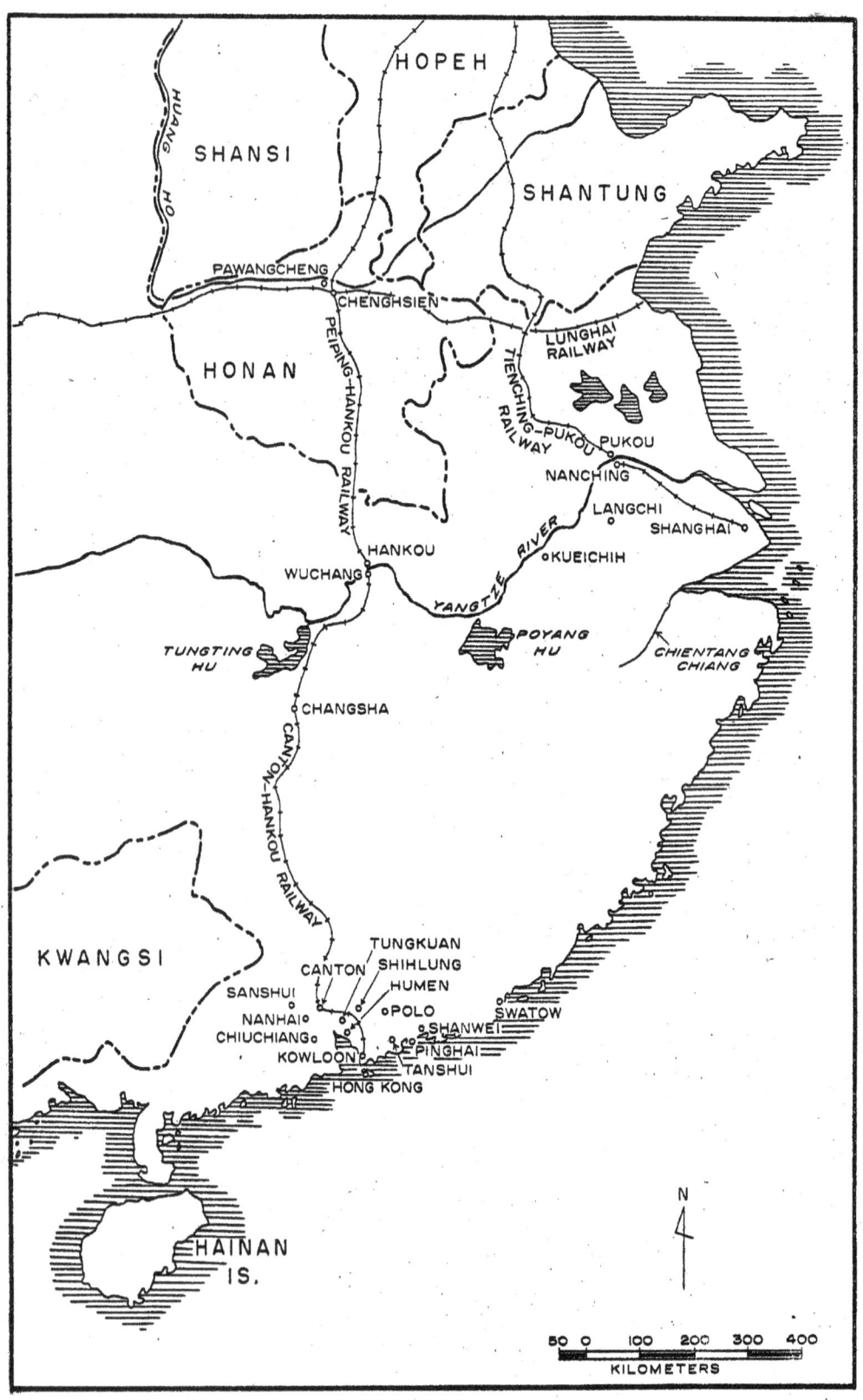

CHAPTER 1

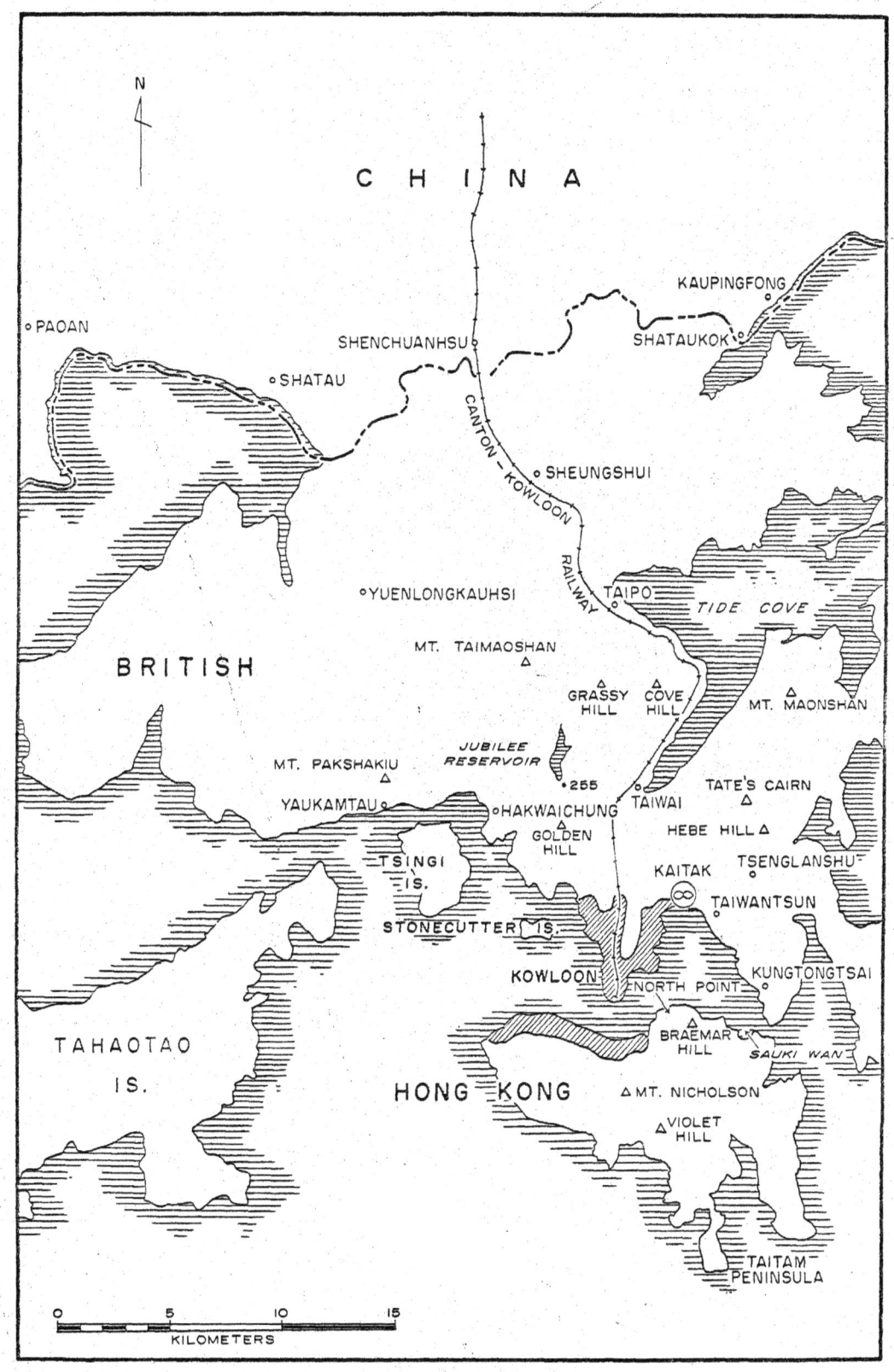

CHAPTER 1

Operations in Chinese Theater After the Outbreak of the Pacific War

The outbreak of the Pacific War did not alter the main objective of the Japanese operations against China, which was the overthrow of the Chiang Kai-shek regime. It was hoped by exploiting the gains in battle in the Southern Area to bring greater pressure on the Chinese and, although part of the Japanese forces would have to be withdrawn from China to be used in the south, all important areas in China would continue to be occupied. Hong Kong would be captured and all enemy foreign influence would be forced out of China by the confiscation of their concessions, rights and interests. Furthermore, it was felt that if military successes were followed by adequate political and administrative measures, the Chiang Kai-shek regime would ultimately surrender.

Such was the estimate of the situation underlying the subsequent plan of operations against China, the main points of which were:

Japanese forces would continue to occupy the zones already under their control and would strive to promptly restore peace and order in the strategic areas of Suiyuan, northern Shansi, Hopeh and Shantung Provinces and the Delta Zone in the lower stream of the Yangtze River in central China, while in the Wuchang-Hankou sector every effort would be made to smash the enemy's fighting power.

Five divisions (5th, 18th, 21st, 33d, and 38th Divisions) and the main force of the air units in China would be transferred to the southern front to support operations there. The 4th Division would assemble in the vicinity of Shanghai and be placed under the direct command of Imperial General Headquarters.

The 23d Army, upon receiving confirmation of the opening of the Malay Operation, would attack and occupy Hong Kong with a force composed mainly of the 38th Division.

With the occupation of Hong Kong, all British, American and other Allied concessions, rights and interests would be confiscated.

All areas where resources of important materials were located would be occupied and the resources would be exploited to build up the Japanese war power.

Situation in China After the Outbreak of the Pacific War

With the outbreak of the Pacific War, the Chinese forces resumed vigorous guerrilla warfare against the Japanese forces but in all sectors the Japanese took the initiative in battle and beat them off.

In North China, in Suiyuan Province, the Japanese Army took the initiative and attacked the newly organized 7th Cavalry Division while it was preparing for action.

Although the Communist troops within the occupied zone of the 1st Army did not take the offensive, they still remained in Shansi Province and continued to harass the Army and disturb the peace.

At the end of 1941 there were indications that the Communist troops in southern and central Hopeh Province would sooner or later assume the offensive but the Japanese 110th Division checked their activities by immediately sending out punitive expeditions to wipe them out. There was no evidence of Communist troops in the eastern sector of this province.

Toward the end of December 1941, the enemy attacked Pawangcheng on the south bank of the Huang Ho in Honan Province but this did not develop into a major action.

In Shantung Province not only were the troops of Gen Yu Hsueh-Chung in conflict with the Communists but the Japanese sent frequent punitive expeditions against both these forces.

In the Wuchang-Hankou sector, on 24 December 1941 the Japanese launched the 2d Changsha Operation[1] and achieved the dual mission of a diversionary operation in support of the Hong Kong Operation and the checking of active guerrilla warfare.

In the sector along the lower reaches of the Yangtze River, on 20 December the 13th Army started its action and smashed the enemy in the vicinity of Langchi, south of Nanching, in the area southeast of Kueichih and on the southern bank of the Chientang

---

1. This operation was known to the Chinese as the 3d Changsha Operation. See Monograph 179, Central China Area Operations Record, 1937 - 1941, footnote 65.

Chiang.

In south China, after the fall of Hong Kong several enemy divisions, which had been gathering in the area east of Canton, gradually retreated and returned to their parent armies.

With the Southern Army's southward advance and the capture of Hong Kong, the 23d Army was automatically relieved of the mission of intercepting the enemy supply lines. Maintenance of peace and security then became its main mission.

In summary, although the Japanese forces in China were reduced to some extent the Chinese did not dare attack them and except for minor punitive expeditions which the Japanese forces made occasionally until the spring of 1942 in north China, particularly in east Hopeh, the southeast, south and northwest parts of Shansi Province and in central Shantung Province, all battlefronts remained quiet.

Maintenance of Strength in China

At the outbreak of the Pacific War, the China Expeditionary Army had under its command the following units:

Land Units

Armies		Divisions	Brigades
North China Area Army	Troops under direct command of the Area Army	27th, 35th, 110th	1st, 7th, 8th, 15th Indep Mixed Brigades

	Armies	Divisions	Brigades
North China Area Army	1st Army	36th, 37th, 41st	3d, 4th, 9th, 16th Indep Mixed Brigades
	12th Army	17th, 32d	5th, 6th, 10th Indep Mixed Brigades, 4th Cav Brigade
	Mongolia Garrison Army	26th	2d Indep Mixed Brigade
11th Army		3d, 6th, 13th, 34th, 39th, 40th	14th, 18th Indep Mixed Brigades
13th Army		15th, 22d, 116th	11th, 12th, 13th, 17th, 20th Indep Mixed Brigades
23d Army		51st, 104th	19th Indep Mixed Brigade
Total		20 Divisions	21 Brigades

Air Units

1st Air Brigade

    1 recon air regt and 2 air sqdrns
        (44th Air Regt)
        (18th Indep Air Sqdrn)
        (83d Indep Air Sqdrn)

    1 fighter regt and 1 air sqdrn
        (54th Air Regt)
        (10th Indep Air Sqdrn)

    1 direct cooperation air unit
        (8th Direct Cooperation Air Unit)

During the battle for Hong Kong, the 45th Air Regiment (light bombers) was temporarily placed under the command of the

China Expeditionary Army and, immediately after the fall of Hong Kong, the 38th Division was transferred to the Southern Army. Furthermore, in November 1941, the 5th, 18th, 21st and 33d Divisions were withdrawn from the China Theater and transferred to the Southern Army while, on 15 November 1941, the 4th Division was transferred to Shanghai.

Although the 51st Division, which had been activated in Japan on 18 September 1941, arrived in China in late October or early November, due to transfers the forces in that theater were still five divisions short, and it was not considered that there was sufficient strength to maintain the status quo. To correct this situation, in early February 1942, Imperial General Headquarters issued an order to the China Expeditionary Army to activate six divisions by augmenting and reorganizing six of their independent mixed brigades. These were activated in April with the 69th Division being assigned to the 1st Army, the 59th Division to the 12th Army, the 58th and 68th Divisions to the 11th Army and the 60th and 70th Divisions to the 13th Army.

In April, after the close of the first stage of the Southern Invasion Operations, the Japanese air units in China were gradually augmented and in early July the 3d Air Division was organized comprising all the air units in China, which were:

    Hq, 3d Air Division

    1st Air Brigade

        10th Indep Air Sqdrn (fighters)
        16th Air Regt (light bombers)
        90th Air Regt (light bombers)

44th Air Regt (recon)

54th Air Regt (fighter)

18th Indep Air Sqdrn (recon)

83d Indep Air Sqdrn (recon)

8th Direct Cooperation Air Unit

Ground Service Units

Hong Kong Operation

General Situation Prior to the Operation

When fighting broke out in Hong Kong, there was a land force of approximately 10,000 British and Indian troops combined and about 10 airplanes stationed in the area. The main defense line of Kowloon Peninsula consisted of several lines of pillbox positions running from Hakwaichung southwest of the Jubilee Reservoir to Hill 225, through Tate's Cairn to the vicinity of Hebe Hill. On Hong Kong Island there were guns of various caliber mounted to cover the shoreline which, in turn, was heavily protected with trenches and obstacles. Furthermore, in the highlands overlooking the city of Hong Kong, lines of pill box positions had been constructed in depth.

Up to the time of the outbreak of the Pacific War no great changes had been discernible in the general conduct of the British concessions or their military installations. However, field maneuvers in the frontier regions were carried out fairly frequently and reconnaissance parties operated along the British-China boundary. About early December, most of the British-Indian troops which had been stationed on the plains of Sheungshui were withdrawn to the main defense positions. When hostilities broke out in Hong Kong, therefore, it appeared as though the fortress was ready to meet the challenge.

Further, the Chinese 4th War Sector Army with a force of approximately 10 divisions confronted at close quarters the northern battleline of the Japanese 23d Army. (Map 1)

Prior to the Pacific War, the 23d Army, commanded by Lt Gen Takashi Sakai, had occupied the area surrounding Canton with the 18th, 104th and 38th Divisions, the vicinity of Swatow with the 19th Independent Mixed Brigade, the vicinity of Shanwei, Tanshui and Shenchuanhsu with the Army Artillery Unit and the northern part of Hainan Island with one infantry regiment of the 48th Division. In the fall of 1941, when the 51st Division was incorporated into the 23d Army, some changes were made in the disposition of troops. (Map 2) The 18th Division was relieved of its garrison mission by the 51st Division and moved its main force to the vicinity of the Canton-Kowloon railway. The 38th Division, after transferring the responsibility for the security of the areas north of Chiuchiang to part of the 104th Division, moved closer to Nanhai and Sanshui. The Araki Detachment (three infantry battalions and one field artillery battalion) of the 51st Division was placed under the direct command

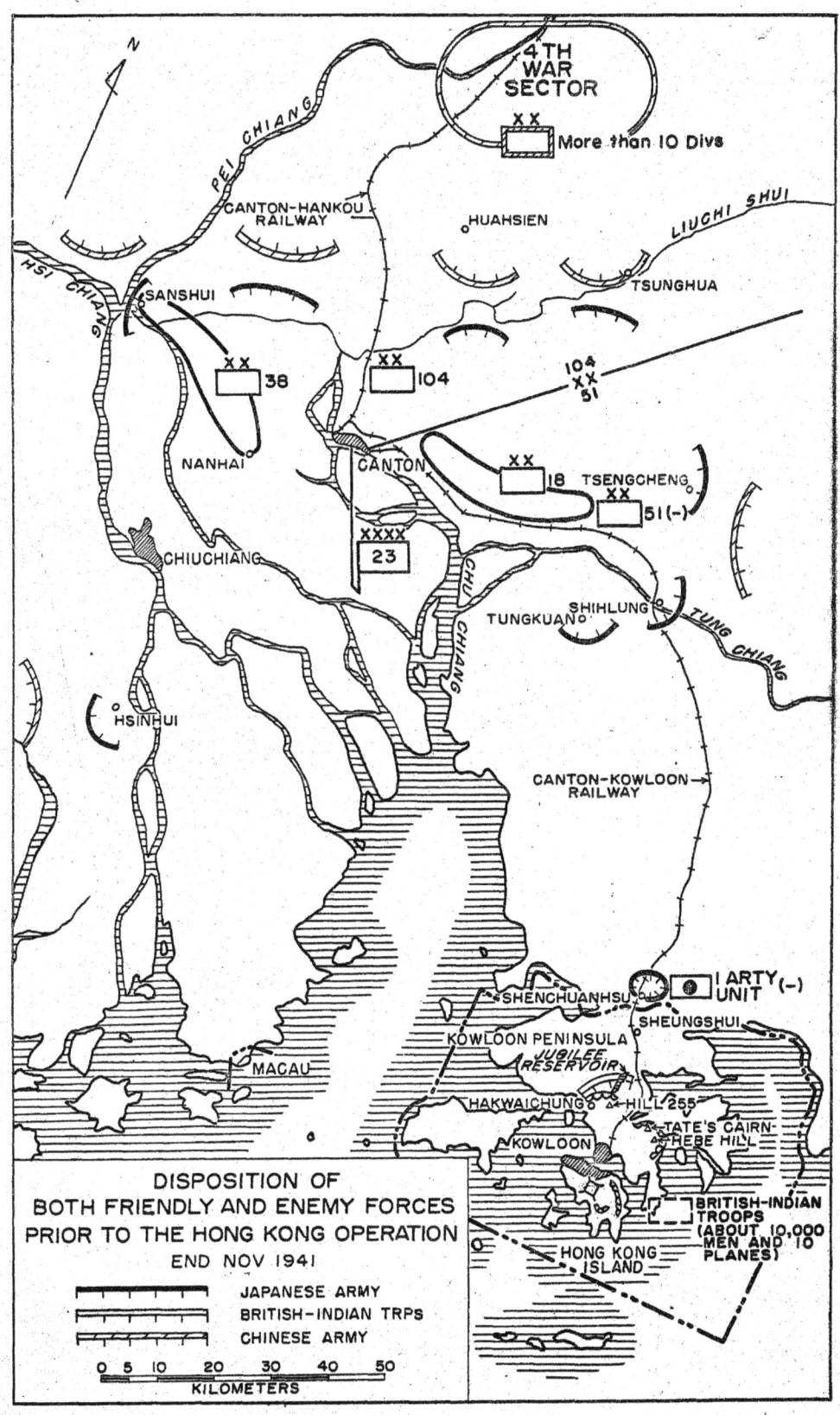

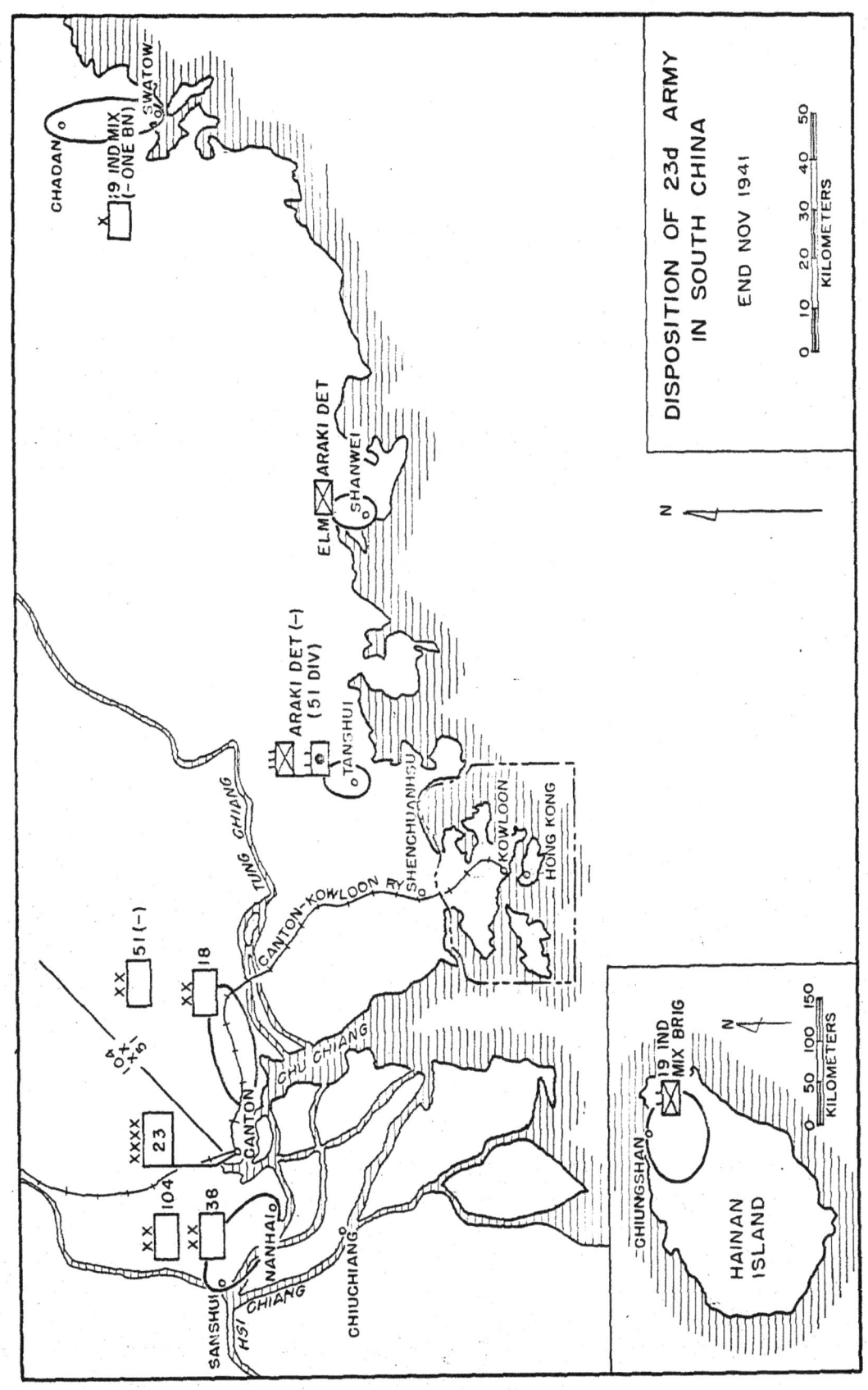

of the Army and assigned the duty of garrisoning Shanwei and Tanshui. In mid-November, one battalion of the 19th Independent Mixed Brigade was assigned garrison duty in north Hainan Island, replacing the infantry regiment of the 48th Division, which then returned to its parent organization.

Operational Command

On 6 November 1941, Imperial General Headquarters ordered the Commander in Chief of the China Expeditionary Army, in cooperation with the Navy, to prepare to attack Hong Kong with a force of which the 38th Division of the 23d Army would form the core. Details of the operation together with the main points of the Central Agreement reached between the Army and Navy setting the time of completion of preparations as the end of November were communicated to him. He was ordered to carry out all preparations in the strictest secrecy.

This plan did not imperil the security of the area occupied by the 23d Army. An attack unit was to be used to strike Hong Kong while part of the Army's force was to check the Chinese troops from interfering from the north.

The main points of the plan were:

Objective:

The main objective of the Hong Kong Operation is to capture Hong Kong by destroying the enemy forces.

Policy:

In cooperation with the Navy, an element of the 23d Army will attack Kowloon Peninsula and Hong Kong Island from the mainland.

Strength:

Refer to attached Standard Table of

Strength. (Chart No. 1.)

In strict secrecy, the 23d Army will assemble powerful units of its attack force in the vicinity of Shenchuanhsu while its main force will assemble in the vicinity of Humen, Shihlung and Canton.

The operation will commence immediately after the operation in Malaya is definitely known to have started.

As soon as the battle has begun, Army and Navy air units will strike Hong Kong and its environs. Enemy air power will be neutralized and all important military installations, as well as all vessels in the harbor, will be destroyed.

The invasion force, timing the action with the progress of the air attack, will break across the boundary near Shenchuanhsu, occupy Mt Taimaoshan and press forward to a line running east to west of the Hill.

At this line the invasion force will prepare for a major attack. It will advance and destroy enemy positions aligned east to west near Jubilee Reservoir and drive down to the southern tip of Kowloon Peninsula. To support the advance of the main invasion force, a small sea advance unit will operate near Tsingi Isle. Then, depending upon the battle situation, troops may be landed to the west of Mt Maonshan in order to attack the enemy's right flank.

Immediately after the capture of Kowloon Peninsula, troops will prepare to attack Hong Kong. Enemy military installations on such small islands as Tsingi, Stonecutter and others must be destroyed before the major operation is launched.

In attacking Hong Kong, troops will first land on its northern beach and from there enlarge their gains. To facilitate this operation, as large a demonstration movement as possible will be staged on the southern beach of Hong Kong to lead the enemy to believe forces will land there.

The invasion will be carried out in close cooperation with the Navy.

If battle exigencies demand, part of the Army and Navy air units already in action in

Chart No 1

Standard Table of Strength Assigned
to the Capture of Hong Kong

Combatant Units

    The 38th Div
    Inf Regt reinforced 1
    Indep Anti-tank Gun Bns 2
    Indep Mt Arty Regt 1
    Heavy Fld Arty Regt 1
    Heavy Fld Arty Bn 1
    Mortar Bn 1
    Arty Intell Regt 1

    Indep Eng Regts   a. General Purpose 2
                       b. Landing & Shipping . . 1

    Air Units Air Sqrns a. Recon 1
                       b. Fighter 1
        Air Regt (light bomber) 1
        Airfield Bn 1
    Signal Unit Comm Regt . . . . Main Force
        Indep Comm Co 1
        Indep Radio Comm Plat 1
    River Crossing Material Co
    Logistical Units
        Motor Trans Cos 4
        Indep Trans Regt (horses) . . . . . Part
        Fld Ord Depot . . . . Part
        Fld Motor Depot . . . . Part
        Fld Freight Depot . . . . Part
        Casualty Clearing Sec 1
        Veterinary Depot . . . . Part

Siege Unit

    Arty Hq 1
    Hv Arty Regt   24cm howitzer 1
    Indep Hv Arty Bn   15cm cannon 1
    Indep Mortar Bn 1

Special Units

    Railway Trans Regt . . . . Part
    Duty Units   Land duty units 3
                   Surface duty units . . . 2
                   Const Units 2
    Water Supply and Pur Depots 2
    Vet Quarantine Depot . . . . Part

other areas, may be called upon to support the
Hong Kong Operation.

Movement after the Capture of Hong Kong:

The 23d Army will resume the mission of maintaining the security of the already occupied zones as well as the vicinity of Hong Kong.
The Army will assemble the 38th Division and other troops in the vicinity of Hong Kong and prepare them for new missions in other zones.

The Central Agreement between the Army and Navy may be broken down into seven important clauses, namely: the objective of the operation; its policy; the time to launch the operation; the main points of the operation; the strength of the troops; the system of command and the division of security responsibilities. As the first three clauses are described in the foregoing paragraphs, there are described below only those points of operation which called for the coordination of the Army and Navy forces.

In strict secrecy, the Army will assemble part of its invasion force in the vicinity of Shenchuanhsu and its main force close to Humen, Shihlung and Canton.
In the meantime, the Navy will tighten the blockade in the waters around Hong Kong and prevent vessels from escaping from Hong Kong or coming to the rescue of the forces there.
At the outset of the operation, Army and Navy air units will attack Hong Kong. They will neutralize enemy air power and destroy enemy vessels in the harbor as well as important military installations.
The Army, timing its action with the progress of the air attack will, at an opportune moment, launch its attack first against Kowloon and then against Hong Kong Island.

> The Navy will provide the Army with the necessary escort force to protect the transportation of Army troops and to support their landing operations. Should the situation demand, the Navy will assist the Army by shelling enemy positions.
> If the battle situation demands, part of the Army and Navy air units in action in other zones will be transferred to the Hong Kong Operation.

In addition, it was stipulated that one division and one infantry regiment of the 23d Army and the main force of the Second China Expeditionary Fleet would form the main fighting body and that the operation would be carried out under the command system of cooperation between the Army and Navy.

The China Expeditionary Army placed three independent air squadrons, three reconnaissance planes and the 45th Light Bomber Regiment of the 1st Air Brigade under the command of the 23d Army and ordered the commander of the 23d Army to draw up an operational plan for the invasion of Hong Kong based on the Imperial General Headquarters' plan.

The objective, policy and time of the operation were the same as those described above. The planned action of the operational plan stated:

> During the Hong Kong Operation, the Army will maintain those zones which it is already occupying.
> As the time for the Hong Kong Operation approaches, the Army will make the necessary rearrangement of garrison forces in order to build up the invasion force which will then be drawn up secretly near the British-China boundary lines. All troops of this invasion force will prepare for action immediately in order that a powerful force

Chart No 2

An Outline of the Tactical Organization of Forces of the 23d Army for the Hong Kong Operation

		Units previously Incorporated	A.T. Gun	Arty	Eng & Bridging Materials	Signal	Medical	Transport	Others
						Units newly assigned			
Attack Unit	Sano Group	38th Div	2 bns	3 mt arty bns, 1 mortar bn	2 indep engr regts 2 bridging material co's	1 radio plat	1/3 of medical unit	6 trans co's 1 motor trans plat	Medical Unit
	Army Air Unit	1 fighter regt & 2 small formations 3 hq recon planes 1 recon unit							1 airfield bn, 1 airfield co
	Kitajima Unit	1st Arty Unit		14th Hv Fld Arty Regt (less 1 bn) 1 mortar bn	1 co (less one plat)	1 radio plat	Part of water supply pur unit	1 trans co	
	Kitazawa Unit	Part of the South China Anchorage Inspectorate			1 engr co				
	Army Signal Unit					2 radio plats 1 wire sig plat			

Chart No 2

An Outline of the Tactical Organization of Forces of the 23d Army for the Hong Kong Operation (Cont'd)

		Units previously incorporated	A.T. Gun	Arty	Eng & Bridging Materials	Signal	Medical	Transport	Others
						Units newly assigned			
Support Unit	Araki Det	66th Inf Regt (less 1 co)		1 arty bn	1 engr co (less 2 plats)	2 radio plats	1/3 medical unit 1 fld hosp Part of water sup & pur unit Part of vet depot	1 trans co (less 1 plat) 1 motor trans plat	Part of each sup depot and 1 fld warehouse
	Kobayashi Unit				1 ry bn			3 motor trans cos	
Logistical Units	Sato Unit	Part of 5th L of C Sector Unit					Shenchuanhsu Br Hosp 1 casualty clearing plat Part of Vet Depot		1 inf co Part of Land Duty Co Part of each sup depot and 1 fld warehouse

may be ready to break through the borderline at the moment these tactics are called for.

The tactical organization of the forces to be used for the capture of Hong Kong are as shown on Chart No. 2.

Actions of Invasion Unit:

Simultaneously with the first attack by the air units, a powerful unit of the invading force will break across the border and attack and destroy the enemy advance units. Then, denying them the chance to regroup, the unit will advance immediately to the strategic line running from east to west of Mt Taimaoshan.

Upon completion of preparations to attack the enemy's main positions aligned east to west of the Jubilee Reservoir, the attack will be launched. The main point of the attack will be the high land east to west of the Jubilee Reservoir. At the same time, the enemy in the Taiwai sector will be attacked and destroyed.

If the battle situation demands, a small advance sea unit will support the action of the main force from the Tsingi Isle sector.

To facilitate the advance of the main force, another unit will cross Tide Cove and aim its drive from the southwestern part of Mt Maonshan toward the northeastern section of Kowloon city.

Should the enemy defenses on the peninsula east of Tide Cove prove weak, the spearhead of the main force may be turned toward that point.

On Hong Kong Island itself, an attack in force will be made on the northern beach. From this point, gains will be enlarged.

If the situation requires, the objective may be attained by blockading Hong Kong without attacking it.

During this operation, the Araki Detachment will withdraw its troops from Shanwei and Pinghai and mass them near Tanshui, where they will prepare to meet any action by the Chinese forces.

The 104th Division will assemble all its mobile forces and remain on the alert against any Chinese attack.

Supplies:

Paoan will be the debarkation base for munitions, which will be assembled as near as possible to Paoan and Shenchuanhsu before the operation. If the situation demands, munitions may be debarked temporarily at Humen.

The collection of war supplies will be completed by the early part of December.

The Army will be held responsible for the transportation of supplies by vessels and motor vehicles. Field supply points will be placed as far forward as possible.

Transportation south of the borderline will be as near as possible to the Canton-Kowloon railway.

The amount of ammunition to be stored at Paoan and Shenchuanhsu prior to the launching of the operation together with that carried by units, must be sufficient for one engagement.

Bridging materials (wood) must be sufficient to build a wooden bridge of about 1,000 meters in length. Bridging materials (pontoon Type B) will be the amount required by one bridging material company as well as 100 collapsible boats Model 95. The materials needed for advancing the operations of the siege artillery must be sufficient to fill the requirements of the Kitajima Unit.

Provisions: Rations sufficient for 90 days for a division. Forage sufficient for 60 days for a division.

Rations and forage must be sufficient to sustain the operational units for a period of 60 days. Consideration must be given to the supply of rations by sea route for the units that will operate from Tanshui.

As soon as Hong Kong is captured the 38th Division will promptly assemble on Kowloon Peninsula and prepare for action in new zones. An element of the 51st Division will garrison Hong Kong.

On the basis of the above operational plan, the 38th Division's operation was divided into three phases: first, to break across the border and advance to the front of the main enemy positions; secondly, to break through these main positions and occupy Kowloon Peninsula and thirdly, to capture Hong Kong.

It was planned that in the first phase the main strength of the advance unit, composed of two infantry regiments and three mountain artillery battalions, commanded by an Infantry Group commander, would break through the enemy's frontier positions from the eastern sector of Shenchuanhsu while part of force, which would embark in landing craft near Paoan, would land at Shatau and advance into the Yuenlongkauhsi Plain. Another part of the force would start its action from Kaupingfong and advance via Shataukok to the area west of Taipo. The main body of the advance unit, as promptly as possible, would drive toward the line of Yaukamtau, Mt Pakshakiu, Mt Taimaoshan, Grassy Hill and Cove Hill confronting the main enemy positions. At this line, they would prepare for an attack against the enemy lines.

The 229th Infantry Regiment was ordered to advance its main force from the sector east of Mt Taimaoshan to Grassy Hill and there await the main force of the Division. The regiment would then assemble in the vicinity of Taipo.

During the second phase, troops that had arrived at the line of Mt Taimaoshan and Grassy Hill would gradually press forward, at the same time preparing themselves to strike the enemy facing them. The main attack would be directed toward the eastern side of the Jubilee Reservoir and then to Golden Hill. After breaking through these points, they would aim their drive toward the southwestern tip of Kowloon Peninsula and occupy Kowloon city. The 229th Infantry Regiment would proceed by landing craft to the northwestern side of Mt Maonshan and, after breaking through the enemy positions in the neighborhood of Tate's Cairn, would advance into the eastern area of Kowloon city.

In the third phase, after Kowloon Peninsula was captured, they would prepare to attack Hong Kong.

The attack against Hong Kong would open with a powerful assault and, after landing on the northern beach, gains would gradually be enlarged.

On 1 December, 1941, after Japan had decided to declare war on the United States and Britain,[2] Imperial General Headquarters issued the following order to the commander of the China Expeditionary Army:

> The Army, in cooperation with the Navy, will attack and capture Hong Kong. The 38th Division of the 23d Army will be used as the core of this force. The operation will begin immediately after it is confirmed that the Southern Army has

---

2. Monograph No. 150, *Political Strategy Prior to the Outbreak of War, Part IV*.

achieved a landing or made air attacks on Malay.
After Hong Kong is captured, the Army will set up a military government on the island.

Concentration of Japanese Forces

Immediately upon receipt of this order, the 23d Army set the invasion troops in motion but, in order to keep the maneuver secret, the troops were forbidden to move in the daytime.

On the night of 1 December, the advance elements of the 38th Division, composed of the 229th Infantry Regiment and the 230th Infantry Regiment which were assembled in the Sanshui-Nanhai area began to advance to the area north of Shenchuanhsu. Advancing only at night, they reached Shenchuanhsu on the night of 6 December.

The Kitajima Unit, the army artillery unit that had been guarding the vicinity of Shenchuanhsu, moved up to Paoan, while part of the Siege Artillery Unit and the Heavy Artillery Unit, which had been alerted at Canton, marching at night, also moved to Paoan. Upon arrival, these units were placed under the command of the Kitajima Unit.

The Araki Detachment left Shanwei and assembled close to Tanshui.

On 5 December, the main force of the 38th Division, together with other units left the Sanshui-Nanhai area, and on the night of the 6th assembled near Humen and Tungkuan. (Map 3)

Progress of Operation

At 0400 of 8 December, the Army ordered its troops to start the

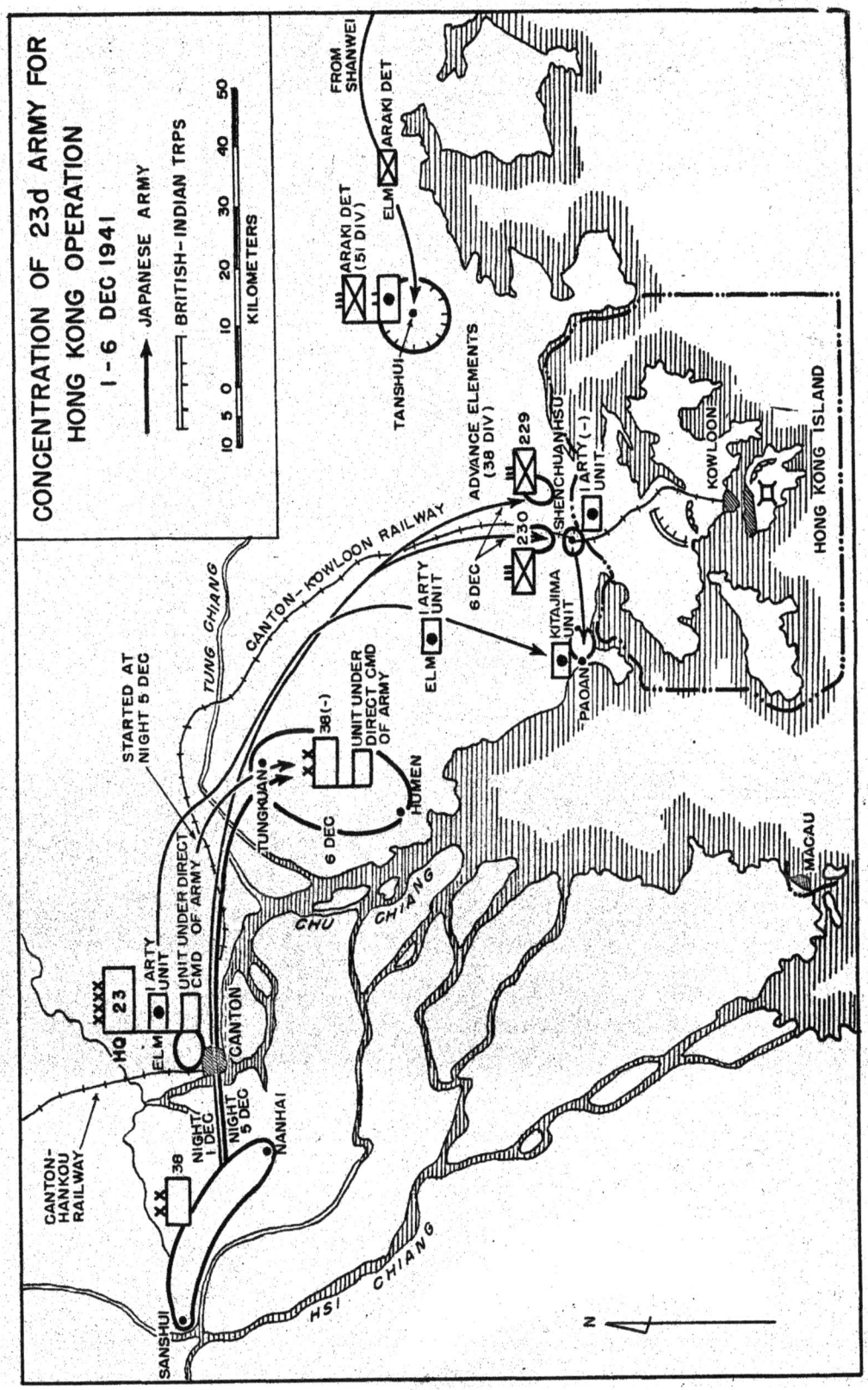

operation. The battle began with bombings by the air units aimed at the destruction of enemy planes and the Kaitak airfield.

The advance elements of the land forces broke across the border and, without meeting much resistance from the enemy, reached Yuenlongkauhsi and Taipo on the same day. (Map 4)

Assuming that the enemy would resist strongly at their main defensive positions, at 1000 on the 9th, the Army ordered the troops to prepare to attack these positions. It was estimated that preparations would be completed within a week. The main attack was to be directed against the high land southwest of Jubilee Reservoir.

The Sano Group was ordered to prepare to launch an attack against the main enemy positions from a line stretching from east to west of Mt Taimaoshan. Part of the invasion force was to strike and capture Tsingi Isle, while another force was to land on the peninsula at a point to the east of Tide Cove where it was to prepare for subsequent battle. The Kitajima Unit was to deploy its main force in the vicinity of Taipo with a partial force in the vicinity of Yuenlongkauhsi. The mission of these forces was the destruction of those strong points against which the spearhead of the attack was to be directed, as well as the overcoming of enemy artillery on Stonecutter Island.

The operation progressed much faster than anticipated. On 9 December, while a reconnaissance party headed by the reconnaissance officer of the 228th Infantry Regiment was surveying enemy positions on the high land of Hill 255, which was one of the strong points of the enemy main defense line south of the Jubilee Reservoir, they discovered loopholes in the deployment of the defenders and using these loopholes were able to capture the positions. This unexpected success spurred the first-line units on to launch an attack against the main enemy positions prior to the designated zero hour and, on the 11th, they broke through these positions without much opposition. The troops assigned to the capture of Tsingi Island made a detour far to the west and, on the 11th, struck and captured the island. Other troops, composed of the core of the 229th Infantry Regiment, maneuvering as a detachment to cover the left flank of the attack forces, crossed Tide Cove on the 10th and, the next day, destroyed the enemy positions near Tate's Cairn. On the 12th, Japanese troops had reached the line linking Kowloon city, Kaitak airfield and Tsenglanshu and, by the 14th, had mopped up the enemy on the entire peninsula.

Encouraged by the unexpectedly rapid capture of Kowloon peninsula, the Army decided to follow this up with an immediate attack against Hong Kong, thus denying the enemy on opportunity to regroup. It ordered the invasion troops to land and, without giving the enemy a breathing space, to storm the whole island of Hong Kong. The main points of the plan for the disposition of forces and preparation for attack were:

MAP NO. 4

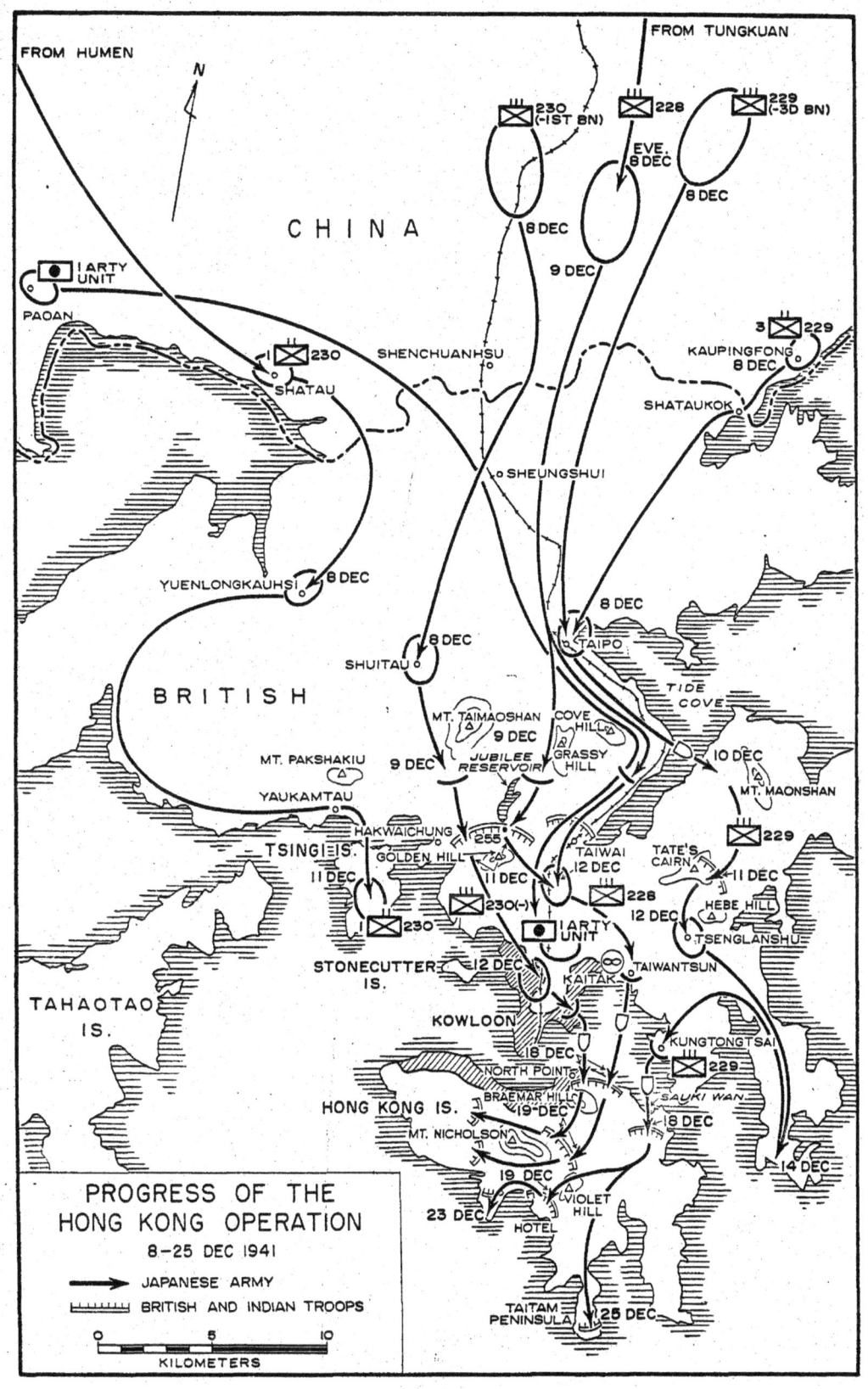

The Navy will support the landing. On a day predetermined for landing, the Navy will stage a demonstration movement along the southern coast of Hong Kong Island in order to deceive the enemy into thinking that the landing will be carried out there.

The Siege Heavy Artillery Unit will take up its positions on the highland in the northern part of Kowloon city. Air units and the Siege Heavy Artillery Unit will support the movement of the landing troops by overcoming the fire of the enemy artillery and destroying their beach defense installations.

The movement of the landing forces will be carried out with the utmost secrecy. The main body will start from Kowloon and Tai-wantsun and land at Braemar Hill. Elements will start from the vicinity of Kungtongtsai and land near Sauki Wan.

Disposition of the troops participating in the attack on Hong Kong will be as shown on Chart No. 3.

Preparations for the landing assaults were accomplished successfully, though not without many difficulties incurred in the transportation of bulky loads of landing equipment and materials. Zero hour for the landing was set for the night of 18 December and this information was communicated to all landing troops and to the Navy.

At dusk on 18 December, the Navy began to maneuver as though they intended to land on the southwestern coast of Hong Kong. The Siege Artillery Units opened fire and smashed the defense installations along the coast to the east of North Point, which was to be the landing beach for the Japanese troops. They continued firing to hold down the remaining enemy artillery.

Chart No 3

Disposition of Troops for Invasion of Hong Kong

	Infantry	Artillery	Engineer & Bridging Material	Note
Right Flank Unit	Inf Group Hq 228th Inf Regt-less 3d Bn 230th Inf Regt-less 3d Bn	5th Indep A.T. Gun Bn 1st Bn of 38th Mt Arty Regt	38th Eng Regt less 1 co	After landing at Braemar, break through the enemy positions on the beach & turn to the right. Adv westward over the northern half of Hong Kong & occupy the island.
Left Flank Unit	229th Inf Regt-less 1st Bn	2d Indep A.T. Gun Bn (less 1 co) 1 co of 10th Indep Mt Arty Regt	1 co of 38th Eng Regt	After landing at Saukiwan, break through the enemy positions, turn to the right with the main force and adv westward over the southern half of Hong Kong. Part of the force will attack and capture Taitam Peninsula
Right Arty Unit		38th Mt Arty Regt (less 1st Bn)		
Left Arty Unit	1 pltn of 229th Inf Regt	10th Indep Mt Arty Regt (less 1 co) 20th Indep Mt Arty Regt 21st Light Tr Mortar Unit 1 co of 2d Indep A.T. Gun Bn		
Landing Engr Unit			20th Indep Eng Regt 1st & 2d Bridging Mtl Cos of 9th Div	
Landing Support Unit			1 co of 14th Indep Engr Regt	
Reserve Unit	1st Bn (less 1 Pltn) of 229th Inf Regt			

Note: Two infantry battalions will remain in Kowloon City and guard the city.

In the meantime, at 2100 on the same day, the 38th Division successfully landed its assault troops and these troops immediately proceeded to drive the enemy out of the eastern sector of the island. The main force of the enemy defenders retreated toward the southern sector beyond Mt Nicholson, where they offered determined resistance. The advance of the assault troops met with many setbacks. The following day, the first assault wave of troops to the right of the right flank came upon a powerful enemy group in sheltered positions with emplacements built into the eastern foot of Mt Nicholson. The enemy fire from these positions was so heavy that not only was the advance stopped but the Japanese troops were thrown into confusion. The left flank units also faced heavy enemy fire from the defenders occupying a hotel on the southern side of Violet Hill and their advance was slowed down. Furthermore, the terrain in this area was so rugged and separated by interlocking ravines that contact with the advance unit was, at one time, entirely broken.

On the 20th, the artillery units of the invasion force landed on Hong Kong and, on the 21st, the first combat line began to recover from the initial confusion.

In the subsequent stages of the battle, the main force successfully overcame the stubborn resistance of the enemy, gradually enlarged its gains and invaded the western sector. Part of the advance began to weaken and, on the 25th, they laid down their weapons.

Japanese casualties during this operation were 675 killed and 2,079 wounded, making a total of 2,754 casualties.

Movement of Chinese Forces During the Hong Kong Operation

Prior to the Hong Kong Operation, the Chinese 4th War Sector Army had more than 10 divisions facing the first line of the 23d Army but after the Hong Kong Operation had begun they maneuvered seven or eight divisions to the east of Canton. One army from Kwangsi Province and the 4th and 74th Armies of the 9th War Sector Army also assembled in the Canton area.

The Araki Detachment (composed mainly of three infantry battalions and one field artillery battalion) assembled its main force in the vicinity of Tanshui. It occupied the mountain areas to the north with part of its force and prepared to beat back any enemy offensives. Although during the Hong Kong Operation the Chinese moved about one and a half divisions closer to the Araki Detachment there was no active fighting.

Administration

Because of the Specific problems involved in the jurisdiction of the occupied zone of Hong Kong, it was deemed necessary to carry out its administration on a basis entirely distinct from that of other occupied zones in China. For this reason, Imperial General

Headquarters favored the idea of setting up a Governor-General in Hong Kong, under its direct command, who would direct the defense and military government of Hong Kong.

On 19 January 1942, the Department of the Governor-General of Hong Kong was created. The Governor-General, however, was placed under the delegated command of the China Expeditionary Army in regard to the collection of intelligence, lines of communication and maintenance of the blockade of southern China.

CHAPTER 2

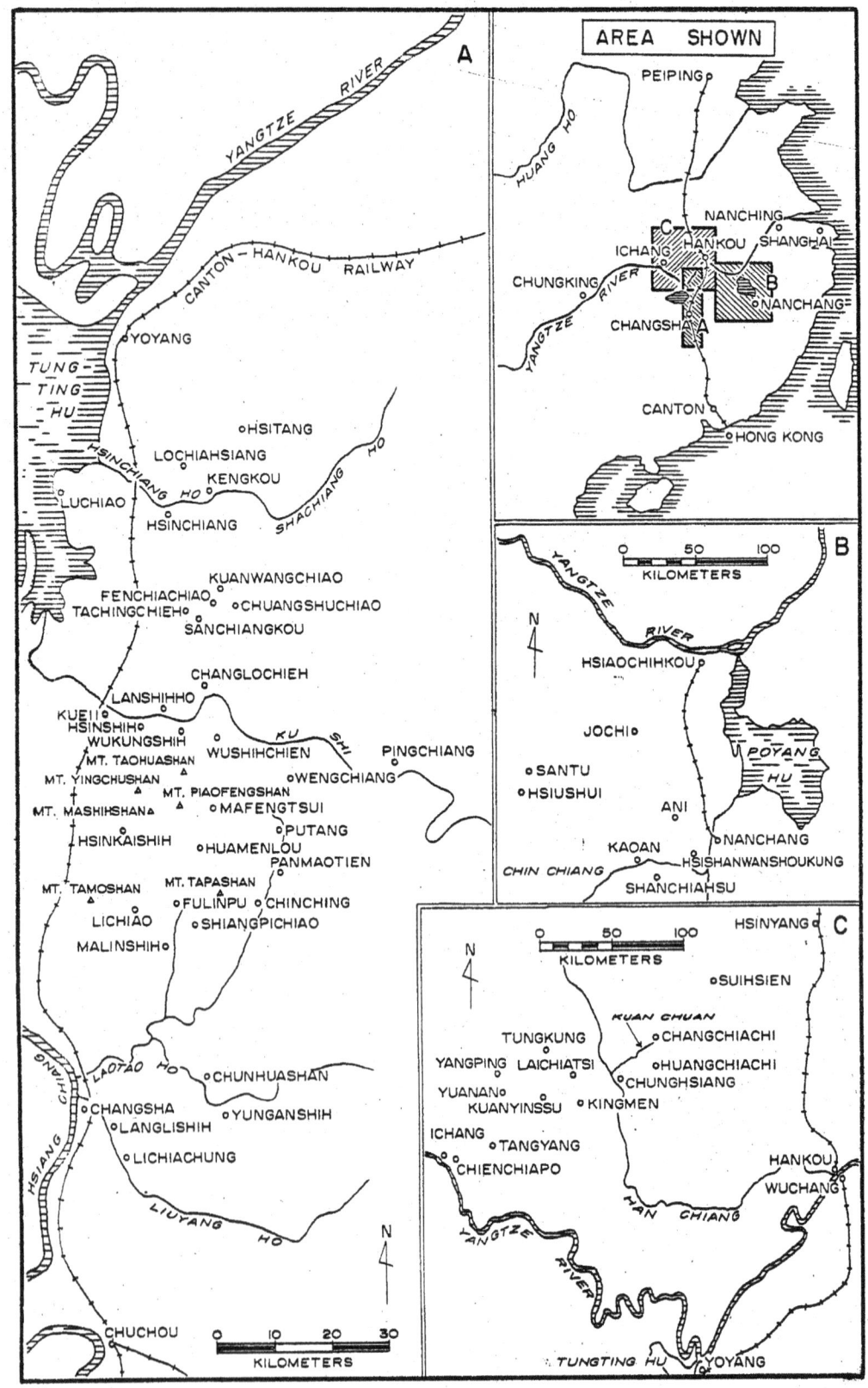

CHAPTER 2

2d Changsha Operation

Situation Prior to the Operation

On 8 December 1941, the 23d Army commenced operations against Hong Kong. On the 9th, in concert with the United States and British forces, the Chungking regime ordered its forces to begin guerrilla warfare against the Japanese Army on all fronts. Some of the Chinese armies moved from Yunnan and Kwangsi Provinces toward the Burma frontier in order to divert the Japanese attention from the Hong Kong Operation and troops from the Chinese 4th War Sector assembled in the areas east of Canton while two armies from the 9th War Sector moved into south China.[1]

To prepare for the Pacific War, in early November Imperial General Headquarters began to draw sizeable forces out of all theaters in order to commit them to the Pacific area. From the China theater, the main body of the air units, five divisions and other units were moved to the Pacific zone. The 4th Division was withdrawn from the 11th Army and assembled in the vicinity of Shanghai and two independent engineer regiments and part of the signal unit were reassigned to the Pacific theater. This withdrawal made it necessary for the 11th Army to redispose its forces. The 39th Divi-

---

1. Approximate boundaries of war sectors are shown on Map No. 10, "Chinese War Sectors, Jul 37-Sep 45," Monograph No. 178, North China Area Operations Record, Jul 37-May 41.

sion and the 18th Independent Mixed Brigade assumed responsibility for guarding those zones previously under the control of the 18th Independent Mixed Brigade and the 4th Division respectively.

The disposition of troops (both friendly and enemy) around Wuchang-Hankou at this time are shown on Map 5.

With the outbreak of the Pacific War, Lt Gen Korechika Anami, 11th Army commander, saw the necessity for assuming the offensive in the zones south of the Yangtze River in order to give effective support to the operations of the 23d Army and the Southern Army. The China Expeditionary Army approved his operational plan and transferred the 9th Independent Mixed Brigade from North China to his command as additional strength. At the same time, it ordered the 1st Air Brigade to support the 11th Army in its operation.

On 13 December, the 11th Army commander ordered the 3d, 6th and 40th Divisions to prepare for a sortie and the 34th Division and the 14th Independent Mixed Brigade, then stationed along the Nanchang-Hsiaochihkou railway, in concert with the main force of the 11th Army, to prepare for battle. All troops stationed north of the Yangtze River began their preparations in anticipation of possible counterattacks from the enemy.

The strength of the forces employed in the main operational sector were:

    3d Div — Div Hq, a core force of six infantry battalions with four battalions of field artillery or mountain artillery.

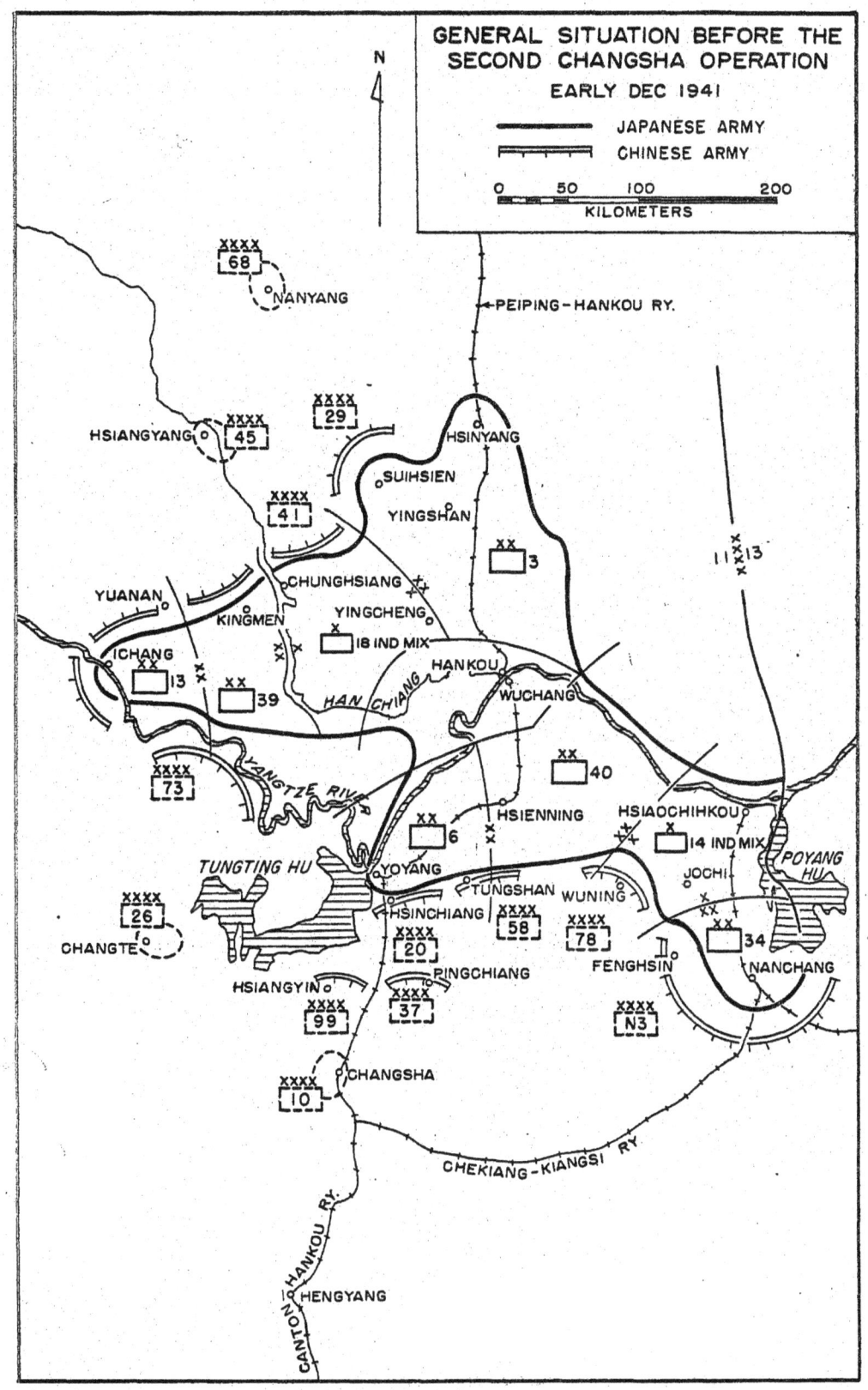

6th Div — Div Hq, a core force of nine infantry battalions with three battalions of field artillery or mountain artillery.

40th Div — Div Hq, a core force of seven infantry battalions with three battalions of field artillery or mountain artillery.

9th Indep Mixed Brigade

— Brig Hq, a core force of two infantry battalions and one battery.

Sawa Det — The core force to be composed of one infantry battalion of the 14th Indep Mixed Brigade.

Tozono Det — The core force to be composed of one infantry battalion of the 18th Indep Mixed Brigade.

Noguchi Det — The core force to be composed of one infantry battalion of the 34th Division.

Eng Unit of the Army

— Eng Hq, the core force to be composed of two indep engineer cos, two cos each of bridging equipment materials and river-crossing equipment materials units.

11th Field Trans Unit

— Trans Hq, the core force to be composed of six infantry companies, one light armored vehicle co, two motor regiments and nine transport companies.

Cooperation Unit

— 1st Air Brigade

After 16 December, the troops began to move into the areas south of Yoyang, in trains, on ships and by marching. By the 20th, the 6th Division had completed the assembly of its forces in the area adjacent to the right bank of the Hsinchiang Ho above Hsinchiang. It then placed its main force forward close to the river and began preparations for crossing the river. On the 21st, the 40th Division reached the Hsitang area, about 8 kilometers north of Kengkou and, by the 22d, was prepared to attack the defenses east of Kengkou.

By the 25th, the 3d Division had assembled near Lochiahsiang, midway between the positions of the 6th and 40th Divisions and, on the same day, its main force began to prepare to assume the offensive. Previous to this, on 22 December, the Army command post had been brought forward to Yoyang.

The 9th Independent Mixed Brigade and the Tozono and Noguchi Detachments were hastily brought forward to cover the flank and rear of the withdrawal operation subsequent to the offensive.

Progress of Operation   (Map 6)

At dusk on 24 December, the Japanese forces began to move. The 6th Division crossed the lower reaches of the Hsinchiang Ho and the 40th Division crossed the Shachiang Ho at Kengkou and to the east of the town. Both divisions then proceeded to drive the enemy toward Kuanwangchiao. On the 26th, the divisions struck and defeated the Chinese 20th Army near a line connecting Tachingchieh and Kuanwang-

MAP NO. 6

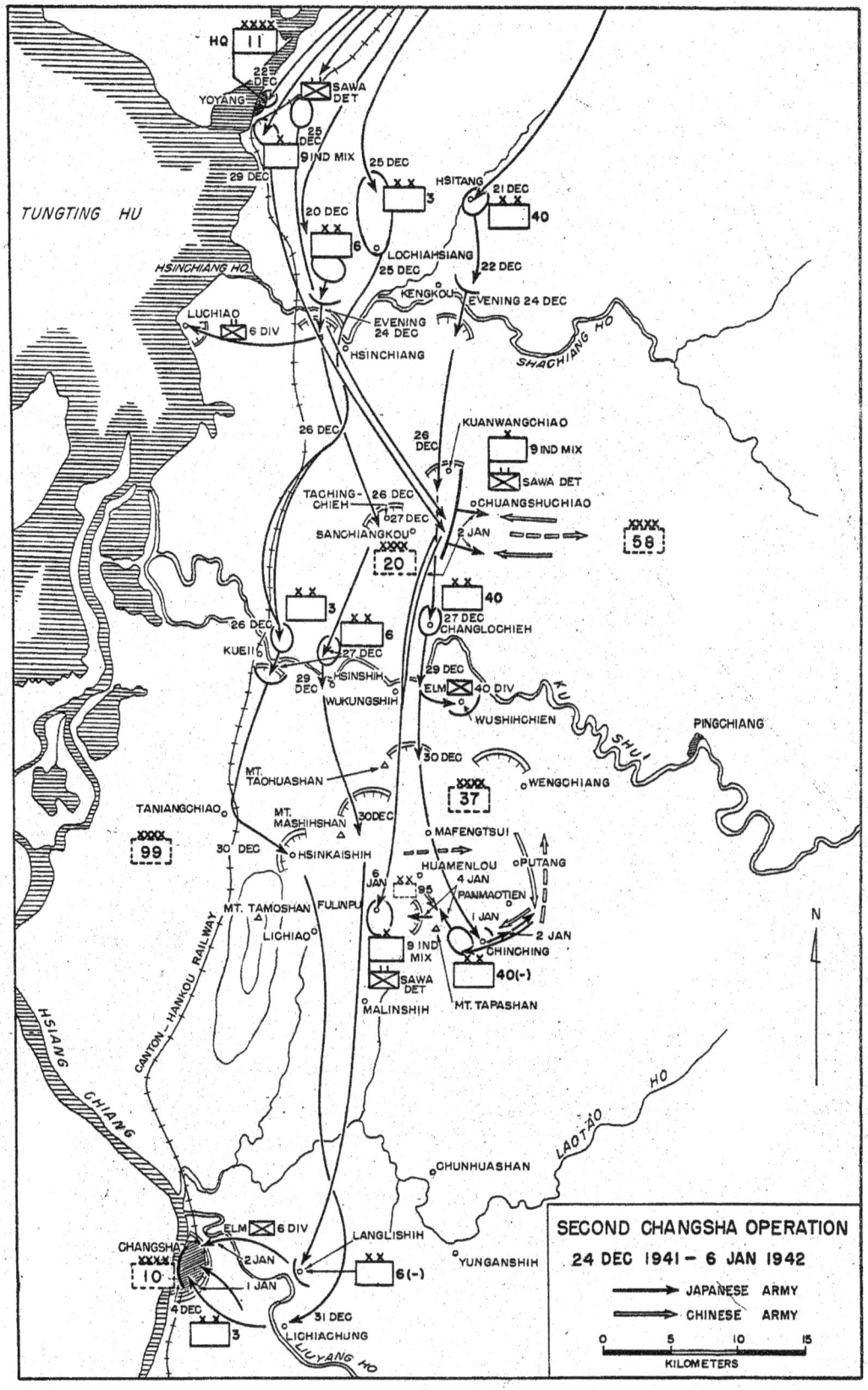

chiao. On the following day, the 6th Division assembled its forces on the north bank of the Ku Shui near Hsinshih and the 40th Division assembled near Changlochieh.

In the meantime, the 6th Division had sent an infantry battalion to mop up the enemy at Luchiao.

At dawn on the 25th, the 3d Division, without waiting for the arrival of its entire force, began to follow the advancing 6th Division. On the 26th, it turned to the right of the 6th Division and marched southward along both sides of the Canton-Hankou railway. On the evening of the same day, it arrived at the northern bank of the Ku Shui near Kueii. Although the Ku Shui was swollen and passage was difficult, the division crossed it and occupied the left bank. Here it met the Chinese 99th Army but easily routed them. At this point the division established a foothold for the subsequent offensive.

The Sawa Detachment, which had arrived at Yoyang on the 25th, was quickly maneuvered to the vicinity of Kuanwangchiao to cover the left flank and rear of the Army. On the 27th, the Detachment, taking the place of the troops of the 6th and 40th Divisions, occupied key positions from the southeast of Sanchiangkou to the east of Kuangwangchiao and covered the left flank and the rear of the Army.

Pi Yueh, the Chinese 9th War Sector Army commander, in an attempt to check the advance of the Japanese forces on the southern bank of the Ku Shui, placed the 37th Army (three divisions) and the 99th Army (two divisions) in well prepared positions running west of Wengchiang to the left bank of the K$_u$ Shui. He also planned to transfer the 30th Army Group (four divisions) from Hsiushui to Pingchiang to undertake a delaying action, but was prevented from doing this by the diversionary action of the 11th Army units in the Nanchang area.[2]

Taking advantage of the favorable position secured by the 3d Division, the Army endeavored to quickly encircle the Chinese 37th Army but was unable to do this because it was found impossible to ford the Ku Shui. The 6th and 40th Divisions, therefore, built bridges across the river and from the morning of the 29th, began to cross the river. As soon as they had advanced to the southern bank, the two divisions launched offensives against the enemy without waiting for their entire forces to cross the river.

The 3d Division was ordered to skirt the northern side of Mt Tamoshan and attack the left flank of the Chinese 37th Army, the 6th Division was to press the enemy along a line running from Mt Mashihshan (12 km south of Hsinshih) to Mt Taohuashan (8 km southeast of Hsinshih) and the 40th Division was to attack the enemy to the east of Mt Taohuashan.

On 30 December, the 3d Division advanced along the road from Taniangchiao (10 km south of Kueii) to Hsinkaishih (about 5 km south-southwest of Mt Mashihshan) and soon occupied the town of Hsinkaishih. In concert with the advance of the 3d Division, the 6th and 40th Di-

---

2. See page 73.

visions attacked and broke through the enemy lines one by one and pressed the main force of the 37th Army back into the mountain regions to the east.

The 9th Independent Mixed Brigade, which had arrived near Yoyang by the 29th, was ordered to guard the left flank and rear of the Army in the area to the north of the Ku Shui. The Brigade rushed its forces toward Kuanwangchiao and, augmented by the Sawa Detachment (which had been placed under its command), on 2 January began to attack the enemy at Kuanwangchiao from the southern section as well as from Sanchiangkou to Chuangshuchiao (5 km southeast of Kuanwangchiao) and succeeded in beating them far back to the east.

After the fall of Hong Kong on 25 December, the enemy forces that had been moving into the eastern sector of Canton apparently gave up their plans to launch an offensive. Japanese intelligence revealed that the 4th Army had been restored to the 9th War Sector Army and ordered to assemble near Chuchou by 1 January.

Changsha at that time seemed to be inadequately defended. Japanese intelligence reported that the Chinese had assigned only a partial force of the 10th Army to guard the city without sufficient relief troops to resist attacks.[3] The time, therefore, seemed op-

---

3. It was learned later that the Chinese had planned to advance the 26th and 73d Armies from the 6th War Sector and the 4th, 74th and 79th Armies from Kwangsi and Kwangtung Provinces to a line near the Liuyang Ho by 5 January. The 20th, 58th, 78th and 99th Armies were also moving south from north of the Laotao Ho at that time.

portune for the Japanese forces to capture Changsha and add to the gains of the present operation. On the night of 29 December, the 3d Division was ordered to pursue the enemy the following day. It was to skirt around the eastern side of Mt Tamoshan and drive toward Changsha. The main force of the 6th Division, after routing the 37th Army, was to advance to Langlishih (8 km east of Changsha) while a partial force was to advance direct to Changsha. The 40th Division was ordered to use part of its force to capture Wushihchien (6 km southeast of Changlochieh) and its main force was to advance to Chinching by way of Mafengtsui (10 km north-northwest of Chinching).

At dawn on the 30th, the 3d Division began its pursuit of the retreating enemy. The Division advanced in three columns, pressing the enemy toward the Liuyang Ho. On the afternoon of the 31st, the left column forded the river at Lichiachung and, by nightfall, the main force of the Division had crossed the river. On 1 January, the Division launched an attack against the enemy in the southeastern outskirts of Changsha castle and, in spite of stubborn resistance by the defenders, succeeded in infiltrating into the castle. However, the three divisions of the Chinese 10th Army that were defending the castle continued to resist so strongly that the Japanese forces were unable to push their drive any further. In the evening of 2 January the 11th Army committed troops of the 6th Division, supported by the 1st Air Brigade, to the attack and besieging the castle on three sides (north, south and east) renewed their efforts to overcome the defenders. By dusk of the 4th, the Japanese forces had occupied all the important points of the city and had finished mopping up the enemy.

By 1 January, the 40th Division had advanced to the vicinity of Chinching and early the following day they attacked and occupied the southeastern highland near Panmaotien (about 4 km north-northeast of Chinching). There they made preparations to strike the Chinese 37th Army which had fallen back to the southern area of Putang. The enemy made persistent sorties out of Putang but was beaten back.

On 2 January, the 40th Division received orders to occupy the narrow passage to the north of Chinching and to assemble its main force near Chinching in order to cover the flanks and rear of the Army. At the same time, it was ordered to prepare for a further advance. On the night of the 3d, therefore, the Division began to assemble its troops in the vicinity of Mt Tapashan (4 km west of Chinching). While assembling they unexpectedly encountered the Chinese 95th Division which was moving southeastward from Huamenlou. While engaged with this force they were attacked from the rear by small forces that were making sorties out of Chinching. By the evening of the 4th, they had succeeded in beating back the enemy that menaced them from the rear and late that night they launched an attack and destroyed the enemy northwest of Mt Tapashan.

On 2 January also the 11th Army issued an order to the Sawa

Detachment to resume its previous mission. At the same time, in order to support the Army's withdrawal, it ordered the 9th Independent Mixed Brigade to move toward Malinshih, 10 kilometers west-southwest of Chinching. Accordingly, the Brigade pressed southward by way of Changlochieh, overcoming local enemy troops who tried to check their advance. On the way, the Brigade incorporated into its command the Sawa Detachment which was following it closely. On 6 January, they occupied Fulinpu.

Reverse Turn After 2d Changsha Operation (Map 7)

As the 11th Army had achieved its primary mission of supporting the operation of the 23d Army by diverting the attention of the enemy to Changsha and driving the enemy out of the major part of Changsha city, on 4 January it was decided to withdraw the forces from the city.

Accordingly, the following orders were issued to its troops:

> On the morning of 4 January, the 40th Division, leaving part of its force in the vicinity of Chinching to cover the flanks and rear of the Army, will advance its main force to Chunhuashan, 8 kilometers north-northwest of Yunganshih to facilitate the withdrawal of the Army.
> The 9th Independent Mixed Brigade will advance to the vicinity of Malinshih and support the withdrawal of the Army.
> The Tozono Detachment (which will arrive at Yoyang by 5 January) will immediately press forward to the vicinity of Hsinkaishih and oppose any enemy force that may threaten the withdrawal of the Army.
> The Army's main force will cross the Liuyang Ho at Langlishih and assemble its strength on the

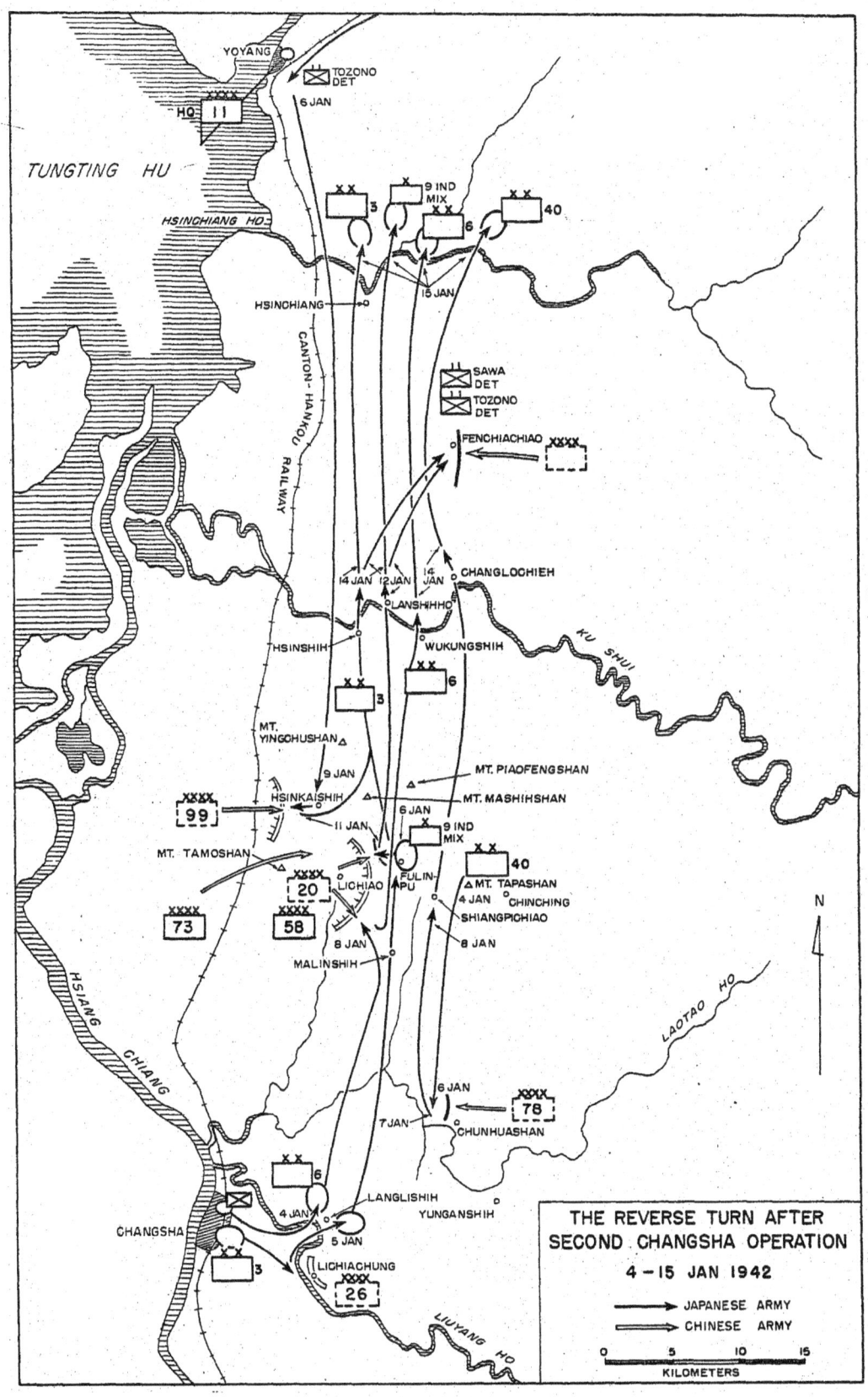

northern bank of the river. The 3d Division will then proceed by the Malinshih-Fulinpu-Wukungshih road, (6 kilometers east of Hsinshih), while the 6th Division will proceed by the Malinshih-Lichiao-Hsinshih road (5 kilometers east of the Fulinpu).

In executing this order, the 40th Division struck first at the enemy on the highland west of Mt Tapashan. By the 5th, its main force had reached Chunhuashan. On the night of the 6th, in order to divert the Chinese 78th Army, it moved into the western sector of Chunhuashan.

The 9th Independent Mixed Brigade reached Fulinpu by dawn of the 6th when it struck at the Chinese 20th and 58th Armies, which occupied the western mountain region of Fulinpu and threatened to cut off the route of withdrawal of the Army. On the same day, the Brigade occupied Fulinpu and successful supported the withdrawal of the main force of the Army.

On the 6th, the Tozono Detachment left Yoyang and by the 9th had advanced to the northern section of Hsinkaishih. There it attacked the Chinese 99th Army and covered the withdrawal of the Army. On the 11th, the Detachment broke away from the enemy. At that time it came under the command of the 3d Division.

The main force of the Army started to withdraw after dusk on 4 January. The 6th Division successfully crossed the Liuyang Ho by a preestablished bridge at Langlishih but the 3d Division was halted in its withdrawal by enemy forces already occupying the river-crossing point at Lichiachung, five kilometers south of Langlishih. The 3d Division retired under enemy fire toward Langlishih where it crossed the river and, by midnight on the 5th, had assembled on the northern bank of the river.

The two divisions then followed the predetermined routes of withdrawal but at Lichiao the 6th Division faced another setback as the enemy had already occupied the town and the 73d and 99th Armies were threatening to enter the area east of Mt Tamoshan, the mountain region west of Lichiao and the area to the northeast. To cope with this situation, on the night of the 8th, the Army ordered the 6th Division to change its course of withdrawal to Fulinpu and, on the 10th, in order to facilitate the withdrawal, the main force of the Army prepared to attack the enemy in this area. The 6th Division, however, with the close and active cooperation of the air units, managed to withdraw fighting its way through enemy resistance. The Army, abandoning the offensive, sent the 3d Division to meet the troops of the 6th Division at a line stretching from Mt Mashihshan, 6 kilometers north-northwest of Fulinpu to Mt Piaofengshan, three kilometers east of Mt Mashihshan.

On the 7th, the 40th Division, timing its movement with the arrival of the 3d Division at the bank of the Laotao Ho, commenced its withdrawal and, beating off the enemy's intercepting actions en route, retired by nightfall of 8 January to Shiangpichiao, about 3 kilometers southeast of Fulinpu.

From the 6th, the 9th Independent Mixed Brigade had been firmly holding Fulinpu, fighting off recurrent attacks from the west by a superior enemy force. With the arrival of the 6th Division at Fulinpu, the Brigade began to withdraw its troops on 11 January and, by the following day, had arrived at the Ku Shui.

The withdrawal was carried out under considerable hardship. Not only did the Japanese forces have to fight off persistent assaults from large enemy forces — from the night of 4 January nine armies and more than twenty divisions had swarmed the battle areas and attacked the withdrawing troops — but they had also been compelled to escort a large number of casualties and rear service units. The enemy, however, relinquished the pursuit near Mt Yingchushan, six kilometers northwest of Hsinkaishih.

By the 13th, the 11th Army had regrouped its forces on the right bank of the Ku Shui, and, on the 14th, it again began to move northward. Fighting off minor attacks on the way, on the 15th the Army reached the northern bank of the Hsinchiang Ho. In the meantime, the Sawa Detachment, which had been temporarily under the command of the 9th Independent Mixed Brigade, after passing Lanshihho, 4 kilometers northeast of Hsinshih on the right bank of the Ku Shui, was released from this control and sent forward to Fenchiachiao, 10 kilometers north of Changlochieh. The Tozono Detachment, which on the

11th had been placed under the command of the 3d Division, on the 12th when they passed Lanshihho was restored to the direct command of the Army. The Detachment then was sent to Fenchiachiao to cover the left flank and rear of the withdrawing Army.

Throughout this operation, the 1st Air Brigade gave very effective cooperation to the land forces, especially in the capture of Changsha and in the accomplishment of the difficult withdrawal of the Army. In the early phase of the operation the Air Brigade made sorties with its 44th Air Regiment (reconnaissance) but after 5 January the whole force of the brigade participated in the operation, affording valuable assistance to the land forces.

Progress of Battle in the Eastern District of the 9th War Sector

In concert with the Changsha Operation, the 11th Army ordered the 34th Division and the 14th Independent Brigade to strike the confronting enemy with their most powerful elements about 24 December.

Approximately six infantry battalions of the 34th Division were ordered to attack the newly organized enemy 3d Army located southwest of Nanchang. By dusk of 23 December, the main attacking force was assembled northeast of Hsishanwanshoukung, 27 kilometers southwest of Nanchang with part of their force in the vicinity of Ani. On the 24th, they started to advance and after smashing the enemy's main positions north of Kaoan, on the night of the 27th captured Kaoan. Using Kaoan and the sectors to the northwest as their base the troops then wiped out the remnants of the enemy in the neighborhood and destroyed their military installations. On the 30th, they advanced farther west, smashing enemy resistance en route, and with part of their strength struck the enemy in the vicinity of Shanchiahsu on the right bank of the Chin Chiang, 15 kilometers east of Kaoan. Having inflicted a heavy blow to the Chinese 3d Army, on 3 January, in accordance with Army orders, the Division began to withdraw and, by the 7th, had returned to its original station.

The 14th Independent Mixed Brigade sent four infantry battalions on a diversionary mission against the 30th Army Group which was then on its way to the Pingchiang area and prevented the enemy from reaching Pingchiang. On 23 December the Brigade left Jochi to strike the enemy in the Santu area. After breaking through three lines of enemy defense positions on the way, on the 29th they captured Santu. Here they fought off persistent enemy attempts to recapture the city and finally wiped out all enemy forces in the adjacent area.

By order of the 11th Army, on 1 January the Brigade began to withdraw its troops and, by the 4th, it had returned to the vicinity of Jochi.

Battle in the Northern Area of the Yangtze River

Assuming that the enemy would strike from the 5th and 6th War Sectors in order to divert the Japanese Army's attention from the operation in the area south of the Yangtze River, the 11th Army ordered its troops stationed north of the river to prepare for battle.

These troops, therefore, took the initiative and made sorties to strike and destroy the enemy forces after decoying them into the range of effective attack.

The 18th Independent Mixed Brigade dispatched three infantry battalions, which were assembled in the vicinity of Chunghsiang and Huangchiachi (33 kilometers north-northeast of Chunghsiang) and at nightfall of 24 December, after driving off all enemy security units on the way, they approached enemy positions established on both tracts of the Kuan Chuan. On the 25th, the battalions broke through these positions and pressed onward to Changchiachi, 35 kilometers north of Huangchiachi. After overcoming the enemy located in this area, on the 27th, they returned to Huangchiachi.

In concert with the operation of the 18th Independent Mixed Brigade, the 39th Division had held a force ready to dispatch to the Hsiangtung area. However, as the Brigade successfully concluded its operation on 27 December, the Division changed its plan and assembled its force of five infantry battalions and three artillery battalions near Laichiatsi, 20 kilometers north of Kingmen and at Kuanyinssu, 25 kilometers west-northwest of Kingmen. On 30 December, this force launched an attack against the Chinese 132d Division and, on the 31st, completely enveloped their main base at Tungkung, 32 kilometers north of Kuanyinssu. This operation proved futile, however, as the enemy had already withdraw from Tungkung. The Division then turned the spearhead of its advance toward the Chinese 179th Division, located near Yangping, three kilometers north of Yuanan. On 2 January they attacked the Chinese from the rear. The enemy fled into the western mountains without offering major resistance. After mopping-up the enemy remaining in the area, the Division returned to its original station.

Around 26 December there were growing indications that the enemy was about to take the offensive. At dusk on 28 December, therefore, in order to take the initiative, the Japanese 13th Division assembled a powerful force near Chienchiapo, five kilometers east of Ichang. Between that date and 8 January, the 13th Division destroyed approximately two Chinese divisions which sought to infiltrate their lines. Although Chen Cheng, commander of the Chinese forces, tried hard to resume attacks he was unsuccessful and the Division continued until the middle of the month to destroy the enemy remaining in the area.

During the latter part of December, a unit of the 3d Division composed of approximately six infantry battalions and one field artillery battalion, successfully pushed back the Chinese 27th Division which attacked them from Suihsien. They were also subjected to several minor attacks from other directions but successfully pushed them back.

The objective of the second Changsha Operation was to support the 23d Army's operation against Hong Kong by preventing the Chinese from reinforcing that area. However, the operation was not begun until the day before the fall of Hong Kong. Under these circumstances, the Chinese were relieved from the necessity of reinforcing Hong Kong and could freely assemble their fighting strength in the Changsha area. In addition, the operational strength of the Japanese forces was one-third less than during the first Changsha Operation and the strength of the enemy had been underestimated. Therefore, during the latter phase of the operation, although they were successful in the outlying areas, the Japanese forces were outnumbered and, in some cases, were overcome by the greater strength of the Chinese. Japanese casualties during this operation were 1,591 killed and 4,412 wounded; also 1,120 horses were killed and 646 wounded.[4]

---

4. Information in regard to operations of the 11th Army in this area was obtained from the memoirs of General Anami, former commander of the 11th Army.

CHAPTER 3

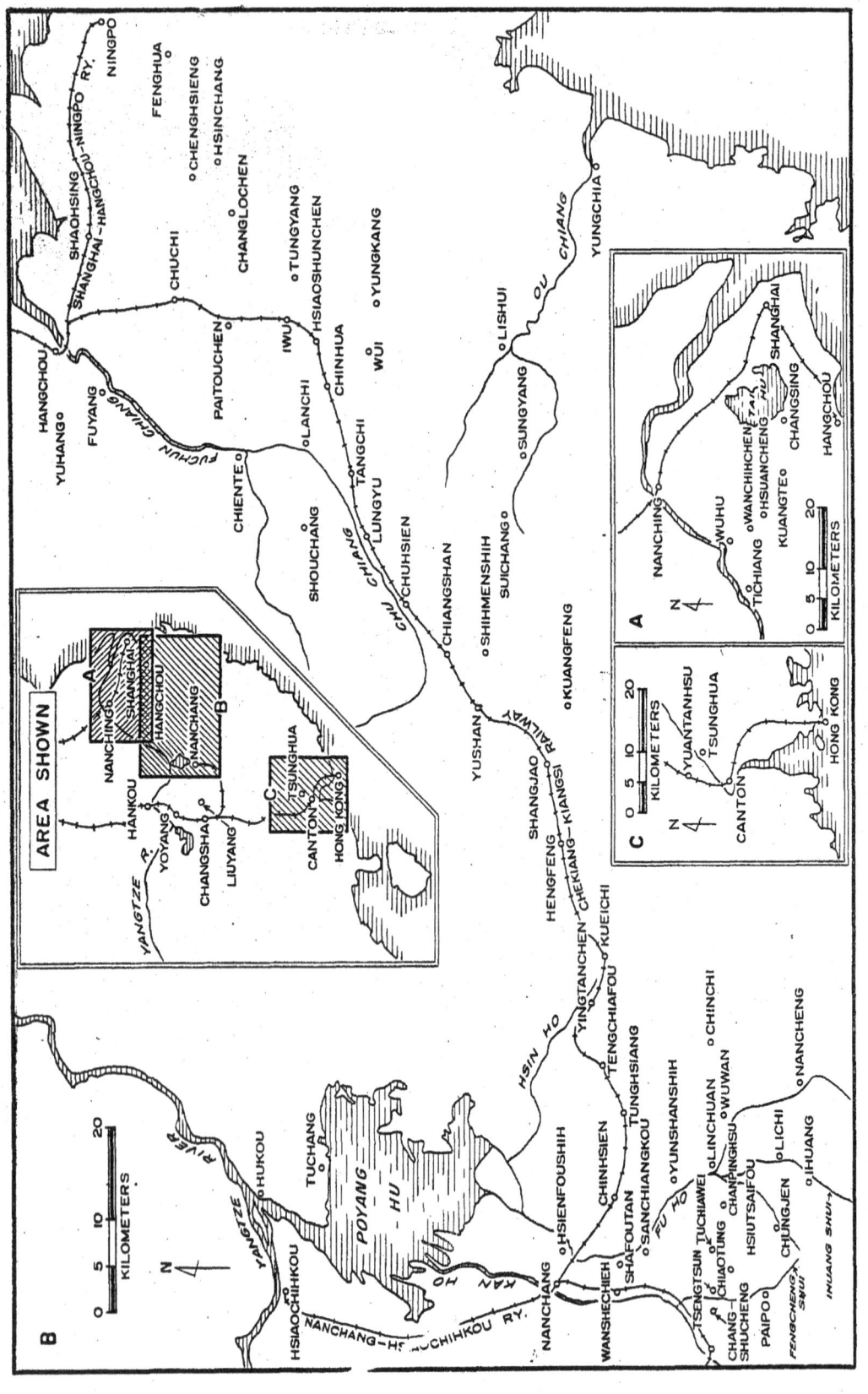

CHAPTER 3

Chekiang-Kiangsi Operation

General Situation Prior to the Operation

The Nationalist Army resorted to guerilla tactics and persistently conducted this type of warfare. During the early part of April 1942 a part of the Chinese 32d Army Group and the 23d Army Group infiltrated the Hsuancheng-Kuangte area facing the area occupied by the Japanese 13th Army. On 20 April, the 13th Army ordered a pincer movement to be begun on 25 April against the enemy in the Tichiang and Changsing areas.

At this time, with few exceptions, the first phase of the operations in the Pacific theater was completed. On 18 April, however, the United States Air Force had carried out unexpected attacks on Japan from an aircraft carrier and, after its bombing run, this attacking force had made its way to the China mainland. Imperial General Headquarters contemplating future raids on the Homeland from air bases and carriers in the Pacific, as well as from bases on continental China, with the raiding units terminating their flights in China, foresaw that air bases in the Chekiang area could be used to advantage by the enemy. It, therefore, ordered the China Expeditionary Army to cease its operations in the Kuangte area and direct its efforts toward the destruction of enemy air bases in the Chekiang area.

The Chinese had disposed the 3d War Sector Army under the command of Yuhan Dou, in the eastern sector of Poyang Hu. With the sudden opening of hostilities in the Pacific area, the enemy realized the great value of this area and sent two armies[1] to supplement this force. The total Chinese strength in the area was then approximately 260,000 men - 33 divisions and three brigades.

The Japanese 13th Army (five divisions and two independent mixed brigades), disposed in the region along the lower reaches of the Yangtze River with the mission of defending the area east of and including Hukou and Poyang Hu, was constantly harassed by guerrilla attacks. (Map 8)

In the Wuchang-Hankou area, the Japanese 11th Army (eight divisions of which two had been reorganized from independent mixed brigades in February 1942) was faced by an enemy force of approximately 94 divisions (the 9th War Sector Army with approximately 33 divisions, the 6th War Sector Army with approximately 22 divisions and the 5th War Sector Army with approximately 39 divisions).

The Japanese Air Force in China did not exceed two reconnaissance regiments, two reconnaissance squadrons and one fighter squadron under the command of the 1st Air Brigade commander. (Map 9)

---

1. These two armies were the 26th Army, which had been sent from the Sixth War Sector to the 9th War Sector to participate in the 2d Changsha Operation and the 74th Army, which had been sent from Kwantung Province to the 3d War Sector to participate in the Chekiang-Kiangsi Operation.

MAP NO. 8

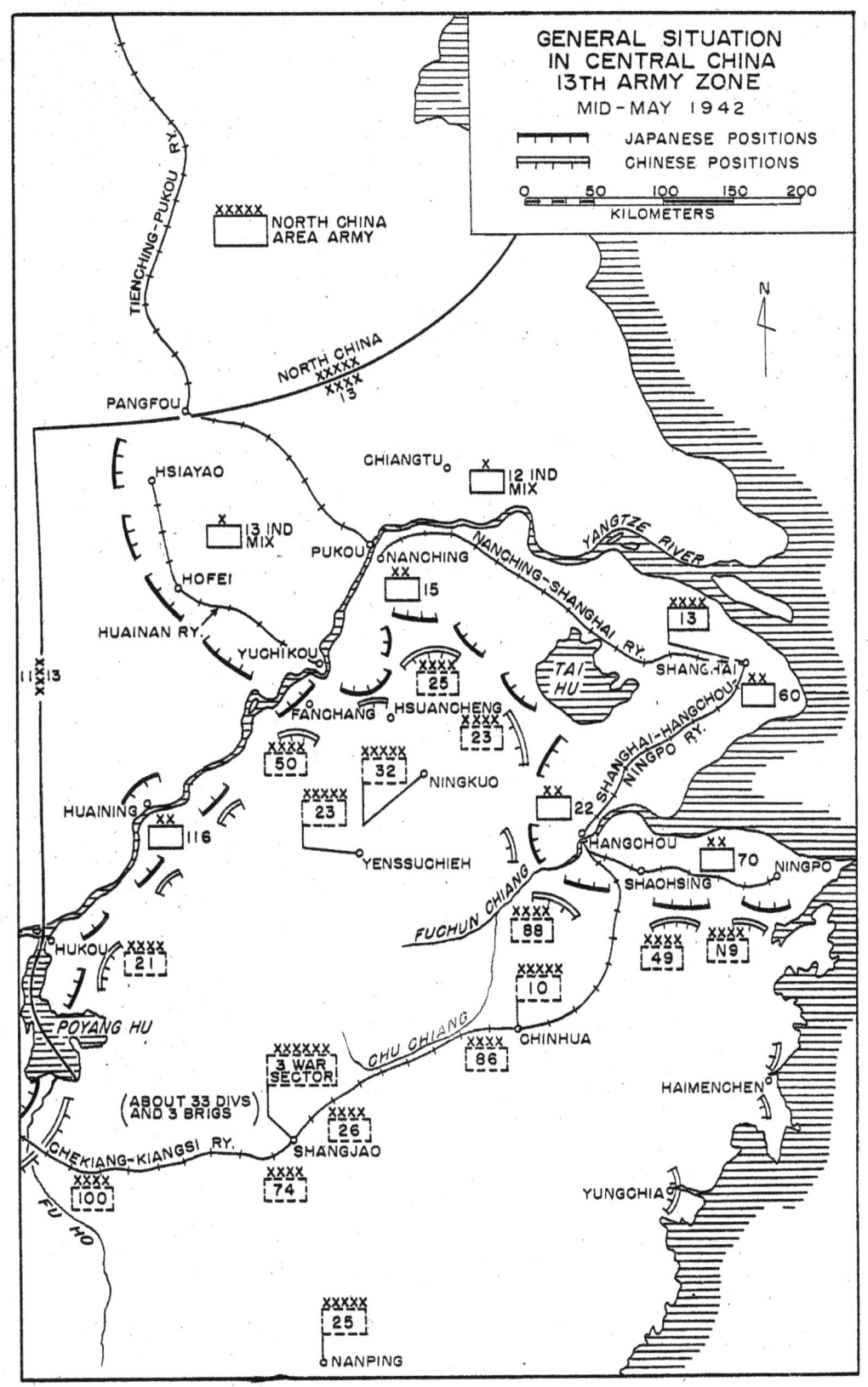

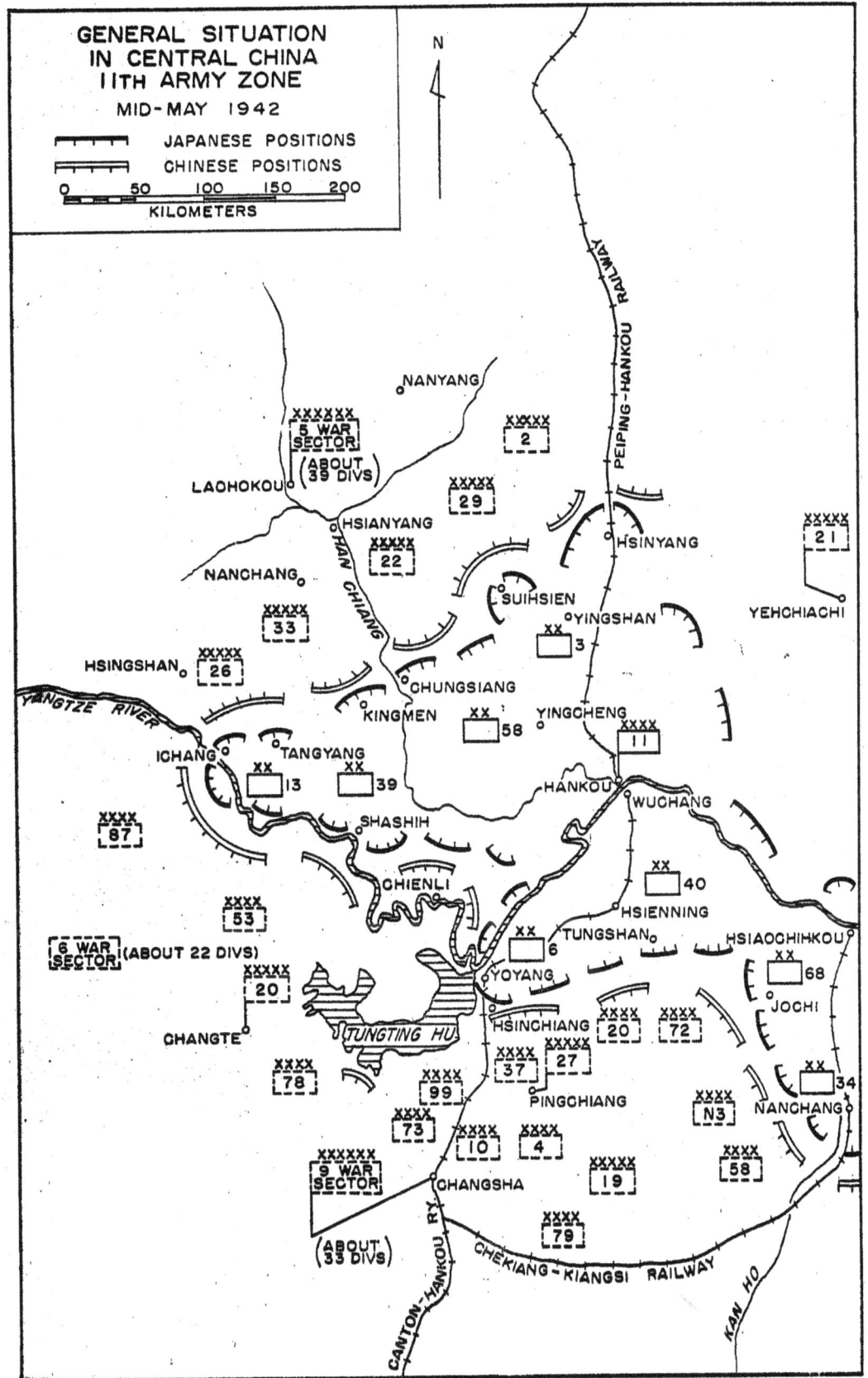

Operational Command

On 21 April, Imperial General Headquarters reinforced the China Expeditionary Army with one heavy and one light bomber regiment.

The Commander in Chief of the China Expeditionary Army desired to carry out operations against the enemy airfields in the Chekiang area after the 13th Army (which had almost completed its preparations) had conducted its operation in the Kuangte area. However, Imperial General Headquarters ordered that the campaign against the airfields be opened immediately and during the latter part of April drafted the following operational plan:

> Objective:
>
> The primary mission will be to defeat the enemy in the Chekiang area and to destroy the air bases from which the enemy might conduct aerial raids on the Japanese Homeland.
>
> Strength to be Employed:
>
> The main force of the 13th Army, plus elements of the 11th Army and the North China Area Army. The total strength of the force will be approximately 40 infantry battalions with 15 or 16 artillery battalions attached.
>
> Operational Period:
>
> The operation will be commenced as soon as possible. It is estimated that the initial battle will be fought during mid-May.

Outline of Operation:

The main force of the Army will attack and defeat the enemy along the Shaohsing - Chuchi-Chinhua road while an element will destroy the enemy along the Hangchou-Fuyang-Lanchi road. After occupying Chinhua, the Army will advance and capture the areas around Yushan and Lishui. Shangjao, the 3d War Sector Army headquarters, will be captured.

The captured areas will be occupied for a period estimated at approximately one month. Airfields, military installations and important lines of communication will be totally destroyed.

Separate instructions will be issued in regard to matters pertaining to the moment of withdrawal.

At the same time, Imperial General Headquarters issued the following order:

The Commander in Chief of the China Expeditionary Army will begin the operation as soon as possible. He will concentrate on the annihilation of the enemy and the destruction of key enemy air bases in the Chekiang area in order to crush the enemy's plans to conduct aerial raids upon the Homeland from this area.

In addition to this order, the following instructions were issued:

Ground units will capture the air bases in the Lishui, Chuhsien and Yushan areas. Other air strips will be neutralized by our air units at an opportune time.

The air bases mentioned above will be secured for a required period of time. The airfields, together with the accompanying military installations and important lines of communication, will be completely destroyed.

Such matters as the time of withdrawal will be directed separately.

Based on the above order and instructions, the China Expeditionary Army drew up its operational plan. The plan generally coincided with the draft from Imperial General Headquarters but called for 53 infantry battalions rather than the 40 estimated in the Imperial General Headquarters plan. Further, it set a minimum amount of time for preparations in the vicinity of Chinhua in order to complete the campaign as soon as possible. The main force of the 13th Army was to commence its attack against the eastern flank of the enemy's 3d War Sector Army from Hangchou on 15 May and the enemy air bases in Chekiang were to be destroyed. Part of the 11th Army, in coordination with the 13th Army, was to attack the western flank of the enemy's 3d Army. The 1st Air Brigade was to attack enemy air bases in the various regions. Troops were to be withdrawn from various sectors to reinforce the 13th Army as follows:

Dispatching Army	Participating Group	Strength in Battalions
13th Army	15th Div	11
	22d Div	9
	70th Div	6
	116th Div	5
	Harada Mixed Brig (17th Div)	3

Dispatching Army	Participating Group	Strength in Battalions
North China Area Army	32d Div	9
	Kozonoe Mixed Brig (26th Div)	5
11th Army	Kono Mixed Brig (40th Div)	5
Total	5 Divisions 3 Mixed Brigades	53

As the 13th Army did not have any mobile lines of communication units under its command, almost all essential lines of communication units from the various armies, especially those lines of communication units under the direct command of the Expeditionary Army, were attached to the 13th Army.

The strength to be employed by the 11th Army during this operation was as follows:

Participating Units	Strength in Battalions	Remarks
3d Div	9	
34th Div	8	
Takehara Det	4	Dispatched from the 6th Div
Imai Det	3	Dispatched from the 40th Div
Ide Det	1	Dispatched from the 68th Div

Participating Units	Strength in Battalions	Remarks
Hirano Det	1	Dispatched from the 68th Div
Total	26	

It was decided that the 13th Army would begin the operation on 15 May without waiting for the completion of concentration of the strength from north China and that the 11th Army would initiate its operation at the end of May.

The China Area Fleet agreed to use part of the Yangtze Unit and Shanghai Area Unit as well as marine units to carry out maneuvers in the Yungchia coastal area and the Poyang Hu area to clear the Chientang Chiang navigation channel of harassing enemy forces and to patrol the Yangtze River.

Preparations for the Operation

The 13th Army planned an offensive against the main force of the Chinese 32d Army Group and part of the 23d Army Group which had advanced to the Hsuancheng-Kuangte area during early April. With the 116th Division and the Kono Brigade assembled in the vicinity of Tichiang (50 km southwest of Wuhu), the 15th Division in the Wanchihchen area (30 km northwest of Hsuancheng) and the 22d Division in the neighborhood of Changsing, preparations for attacking the enemy in the Hsuancheng-Kuangte area were almost completed.

However, on 22 April, three days before the attack was to be launched, Imperial General Headquarters ordered this operation be suspended and preparations undertaken for an attack on enemy airfields in the Chekiang area.

As it was necessary to undertake this latter operation with the utmost speed, it was not possible to work out detailed plans ahead of time. At the end of April, the 13th Army began to concentrate its forces around Hangchou and to the east of that city and, by 13 May, had assembled approximately four divisions and the Kono Brigade in this area. Units from the North China Area Army were unable to concentrate their forces by 13 May and concentration continued after the commencement of the operation. Combat units from the north completed their concentration on 23 May.

From 5 May, part of the 11th Army conducted the Mienyang Operation, approximately 100 km west by southwest of Hankou. It routed the Chinese 128th Division and then prepared for a diversionary attack to assist the Chekiang-Kiangsi Operation.

To assist the 11th Army which was assembling its forces in order to take the offensive, about mid-May the 6th Division launched a diversionary attack in the Yoyang area. About 27 May, the Army completed the first phase of the concentration of its attacking force.

The 1st Air Brigade had been ordered to attack the airfields in the Chekiang area. In order to reinforce the Brigade, in early

April, the Southern Army was ordered to send the 62d Heavy and 90th Light Bomber Regiments to central China. These bomber regiments arrived at the end of April and proceeded to bomb the enemy airfields.

The 23d Army in south China prepared to launch a diversionary attack in the Tsunghua and Yuantanhsu areas in coordination with the initial offensive of the 11th Army in the Chekiang-Kiangsi Operation.

Progress of 13th Army's Operation

Prior to 13 May, the 13th Army had deployed four divisions and one brigade in an area of approximately 150 km extending from Yuhang to Fenghua. The 32d Division, which had been somewhat dilatory with its unit concentration, was disposed as the Army's rear right flank.

It was understood that orders had been issued to the Chinese 3d War Sector Army to "diminish the Japanese fighting strength by continuously resisting attacks while at the same time drawing in, encircling and annihilating their offensive force in a decisive battle in the Chuhsien sector." Their lines appeared to consist of three fortified regions: the first positions were in the vicinity of Iwu, the second formed the Lanchi-Chinhua line and the third were in the vicinity of Chuhsien.

On 11 May, the Army decided to advance its main force to south of Chuchi and southwest of Chenghsien by dusk on the 18th, in order to destroy the enemy in the fortified regions of Iwu, Paitouchen (30 km north of Iwu) and Changlochen (40 km northeast of Iwu). The

116th Division was ordered to advance along the Fuchun Chiang.

On 15 May the initial offensive was launched and progressed faster than had been anticipated. Under the circumstances it was decided that the 22d Division would begin to deploy its forces from the 19th in order to be prepared for an attack on enemy positions in the vicinity of Iwu. With the retreat of the Chinese Provisional 9th Army in the Changlochen area, however, the 13th Army ordered that preparations be begun on the evening of the 18th to rout the Chinese main strength in the vicinity of Iwu and in the area east of Chinhua. The 22d Division opened its attack ahead of time at 1600 hours on the 18th and the various other divisions began attacking at dawn on the 19th. By the evening of the 22d the Japanese forces had occupied the sector to the east of Chinhua and the enemy had gathered its remaining force to strengthen the defense positions in the Chinhua-Lanchi area. (Map 10)

The 13th Army shifted its weight to the right flank and decided again to attack the enemy. The advance of the 116th and 32d Divisions into the area south of Chiente was accelerated. The 15th Division was moved from the Chinhua front to the Lanchi front and the 70th Division was moved from the left flank to the Chinhua front. Each Division proceeded as ordered and, on the night of the 24th, the 116th Division assembled to the south of Chiente, the 15th Division to the north of Lanchi and the 70th Division to the west of

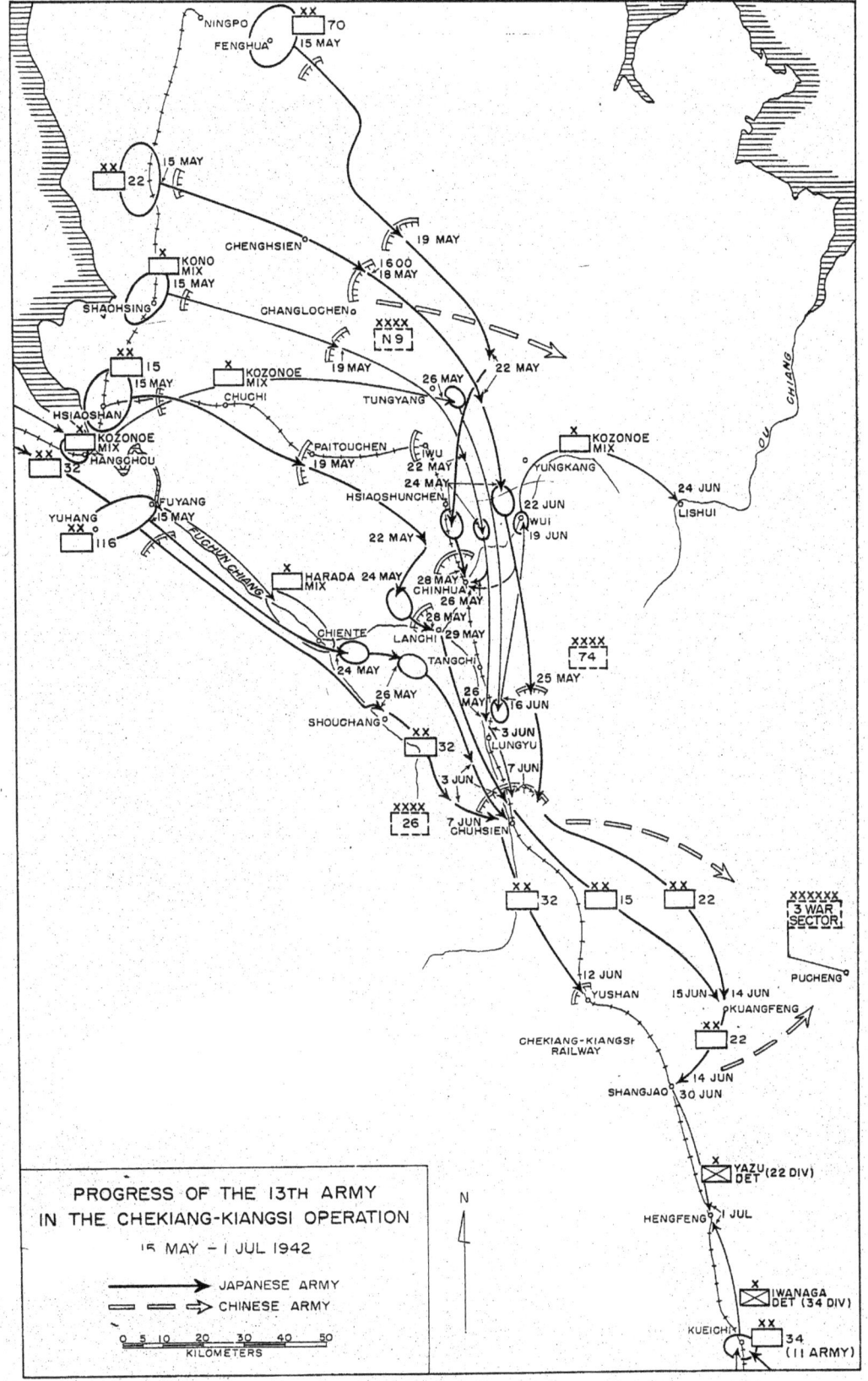

Hsiaoshunchen. The 22d Division then moved to the mountain line north of Wui and prepared to launch its attack, while the Kono Brigade, in the area southeast of Chinhua, prepared to pursue the enemy.

Reports gathered from reconnaissance planes and other sources after 23 May indicated that the enemy had started to retreat and had no intention of making any major resistance. On the evening of the 24th, therefore, the Army decided to pursue the enemy toward Chuhsien without halt in order to force a decisive battle. The 32d Division, which had been disposed on the right flank of the 116th Division from 23 May, faced the southwest and, on the night of the 26th, crossed the Fuchun Chiang in a northeasterly direction from Shouchang. On the 25th, the 116th Division completed fording the Fuchun Chiang and, on the 26th, advanced into the area northwest of Lanchi.

On the 25th, the 15th Division began its attack on the enemy stronghold at Lanchi and, on the afternoon of the same day, the 70th Division attacked the enemy in Chinhua. The Kono Mixed Brigade advanced into the region east of Lungyu. Also, on the 25th, the 22d Division captured enemy positions in the area southeast of Tangchi.

While the battle situation on the left wing was extremely favorable, enemy resistance on the Chinhua and Lanchi fronts had been underestimated. Believing that there was a great possibility of capturing the enemy in this area, at 1300 on the 26th, the 13th Army ordered its forces to "capture the isolated enemy in the Chinhua-Lanchi region and simultaneously to continue the pursuit." Two infantry battalions from the 22d Division and two from the Kono Mixed Brigade (both left wing units) were ordered to proceed toward Chinhua and cooperate with the 70th Division in capturing the town.

In view of the fact that the 3d War Sector Army had concentrated its main force in the vicinity of Chuhsien, the 13th Army ordered a change from pursuit of the enemy to an attack on prepared positions in the vicinity of Lungyu.

In order to capture the enemy fleeing from Chinhua to the south and to prepare for the operation against Lishui, the Kozonoe Mixed Brigade was directed to mop up the enemy in the Yungkang and Wui areas. However, the Brigade was delayed in assembling and did not reach the area south of Tungyang until 26 May. On the 28th, Lanchi and Chinhua capitulated. On the 29th, the 70th Division was ordered to garrison the Lanchi area and the 15th Division was ordered to move toward the area north of Lungyu. Other divisions had already advanced to the Lungyu sector.

At this time, the 70th Division was responsible for the security of the sectors along the Chekiang-Kiangsi railway, east of

Lungyu and Chinhua, while the Harada Brigade was responsible for the security of the Fuchun Chiang area.

The main force of the 3d War Sector Army had concentrated its forces in the neighborhood of Chuhsien and it was evident that the enemy intended to resist stubbornly in this area.

The Army massed its main force on the left wing and planned to capture Chuhsien by penetrating the enemy positions from both sides of the town, thus capturing and annihilating the enemy with one stroke. The 32d and 116th Divisions were ordered to launch attacks from the right wing, that is, from the north of Chuhsien while the Kono Mixed Brigade and the 15th and 22d Divisions were to launch attacks from the central and left wings. The Kozonoe Mixed Brigade was sent to the Lungyu area (temporarily suspending the Lishui Operation) to prepare for flank attacks from the enemy's 26th Army in the north and the 74th Army in the south.

The initial attack was to begin on 3 June. The Japanese forces were instructed to move forward on the 1st and to have attack preparations completed by the night of the 2d.

The attack, as planned, commenced on 3 June. The battle situation progressed favorably and, on the 4th, the enemy was completely encircled. However, during the night of the 4th there was a sudden heavy downpour of rain which swelled the rivers and enemy reinforcements appeared to arrive from the south and the southwest. In spite of this and the fact that the enemy resisted stubbornly, on 7 June Chuhsien was captured.

The Army then decided to pursue the enemy toward Kuangfeng. The Kono Brigade and the 116th Division concentrated their troops in the vicinity of Chuhsien while the 32d, 15th and 22d Divisions pursued the enemy. Although the flood retarded the progress of the pursuit, on 12 June the 32d Division seized Yushan. At dawn on the 14th, the 22d Division captured Kuangfeng and that night occupied Shangjao. On the 15th, in accordance with Army orders, the 15th Division occupied Kuangfeng.

On 20 May, in concert with the principal operation of capturing Chuhsien, the Army planned to use the Kozonoe Brigade to attack and capture Lishui. During the operation to capture Chuhsien the Lishui Operation was halted temporarily. On 16 June, subsequent to the successful capture of Chuhsien, the Brigade advanced toward Lishui. At this time, the 70th Division was deployed to protect the rear of the advancing Brigade. On the 19th, the Brigade assembled near Wui. On the 22d, it left this area and on the 24th captured Lishui and its airfield. At this time the 70th Division dispatched an infantry battalion to both Wui and Yungkang to serve as a rear guard.

On 12 June, the Commander in Chief of the China Expeditionary

Army reported the capture of Yushan and Nancheng to Imperial General Headquarters and recommended that the Chekiang-Kiangsi Operation now be undertaken in order to inflict a heavy blow on the enemy. Imperial General Headquarters concurred and instructed the Commander in Chief of the China Expeditionary Army to "conduct the operation in the region east of Nanchang and, if necessary, along the Chekiang-Kiangsi railroad." On 30 June, the Yazu Detachment (two infantry battalions as a nucleus and commanded by Maj Gen Yazu) left Shangjao. On 1 July, having penetrated the forces confronting it, the Yazu Detachment joined the Iwanaga Detachment of the 11th Army at Hengfeng.

The Navy closely cooperated with the Army to keep the lines of communication clear by sweeping mines from the Fuchun Chiang and by carrying out diversionary actions along the entire coast of central and southern China.

Progress of the 11th Army's Operation

On 27 May, the 11th Army had staged the first phase of the concentration of its main force in the region along the left bank of the Kan Ho but just before launching the offensive the assembly area was shifted to the right bank of the river. The Imai and Ide Detachments were concentrated at Wanshechieh, the 3d Division at Shafoutan and the 34th Division in the neighborhood of Hsiehfoushih.

The enemy southeast of Nanchang had deployed three garrison

groups (militia) in Kiangsi Province between the Kan Ho and the Fu Ho and the 100th Army on the right bank of the Fu Ho.

On 31 May, after sunset the Japanese forces began fording the Fu Ho from the concentration area of the second phase and defeated the enemy on both banks of the river. By night of 3 June, the Army had advanced to a line linking Chinhsien, Yunshanshih and the western Linchuan Mountains. The enemy, without putting up effective resistance, retreated to the south and southeast. (Map 11)

The Chinese 79th Army of the 9th War Sector Army had crossed the Kan Ho and advanced in an easterly direction. On 4 June they assembled at and in the region southwest of Linchuan. Estimating that this army might try to join forces with the 3d War Sector Army, the 11th Army decided to destroy the 79th Army in the region southwest of Linchuan. On 3 June, the Iwanaga Detachment, with three infantry battalions of the 34th Division as its nucleus, was placed under the direct control of the 11th Army. The Detachment moved along the Chekiang-Kiangsi railway and directed its attack against Tunghsiang. The main force of the 11th Army was so disposed as to make possible the shifting of men to the left bank of the Fu Ho. On the 4th, therefore, the Imai and Ide Detachments suppressed enemy activities in the Yinchihsu and Chanpinghsu areas and, on the night of the same day, the 3d Division routed the enemy and captured Linchuan. On the night of 5 June, the 34th Division and the Takehara Detachment advanced to the area south of Sanchiangkou. Al-

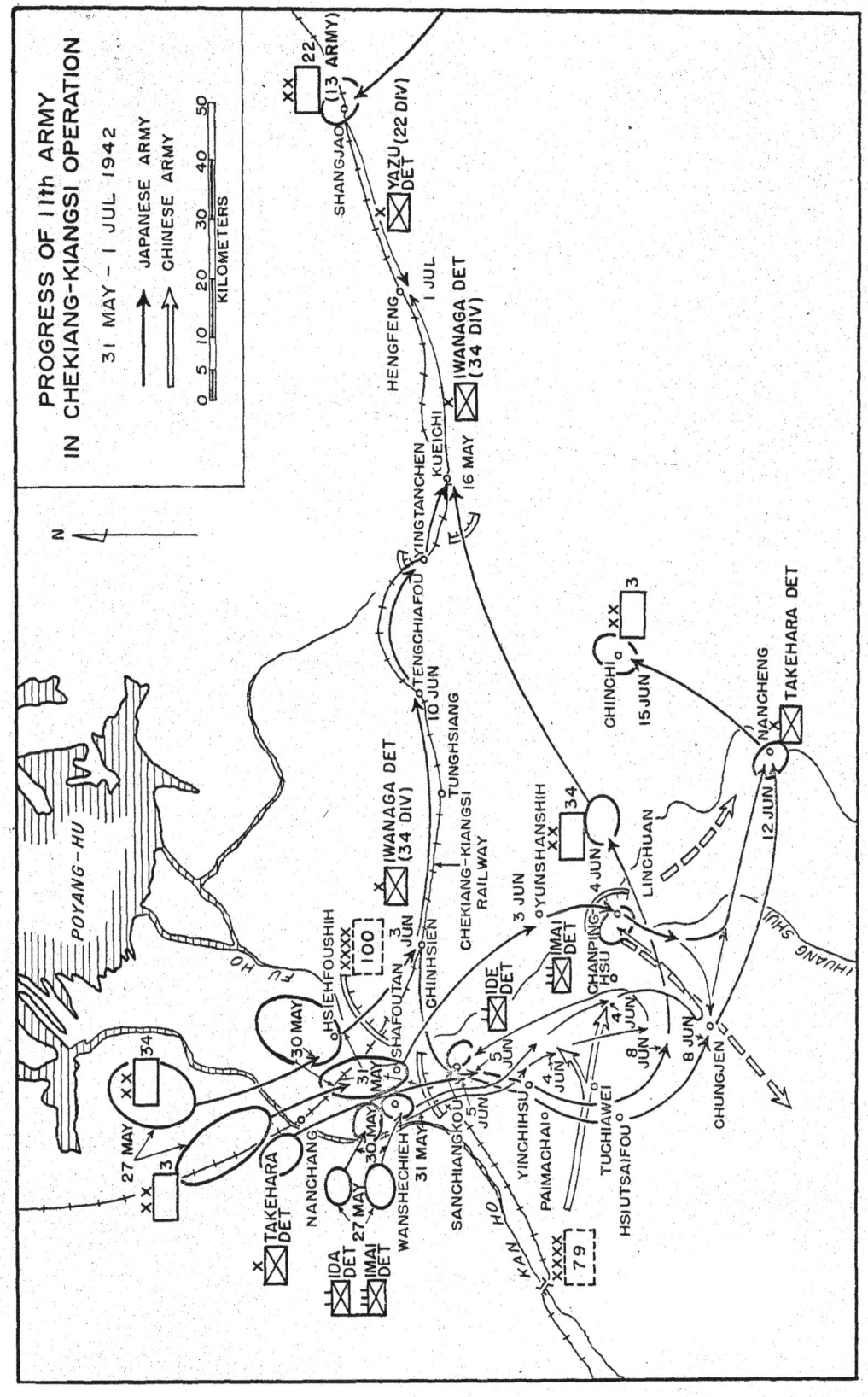

though part of the Chinese 79th Army was annihilated in the area around Linchuan its main force was believed to be located in Hsiutsaifou and the region between Linchuan and Chungjen. Therefore, the 79th Army's escape routes to the west and southwest were severed and 11th Army units deployed to destroy the enemy's main force southwest of Chanpinghsu. The 3d Division advanced along the left bank of the Ihuang Shui from Linchuan and, cooperating with the Imai Detachment, wiped out the enemy in that area. On the 8th, part of the division severed the enemy escape routes in the area around Chungjen. The main force of the 34th Division, reinforced by the Ide Detachment upon its arrival at Sanchiangkou, together with the Takehara Detachment, advanced to the area southwest of the Paimachai-Tuchiawei line, thus cutting off the enemy's escape route in this region. Between 6 and 8 June, the 79th Army was defeated in the sector between Chungjen and Linchuan on the west bank of the Ihuang Shui.

On 7 June, the 13th Army captured Chuhsien and then prepared to attack Shangjao. Realizing the importance of occupying Nancheng and Yingtanchen at this time, on the night of 9 June the China Expeditionary Army ordered the 11th Army to capture these points. Thereupon, the 11th Army ordered the 3d Division and the Takehara Detachment to pursue the enemy toward Nancheng. After mopping up the enemy forces remaining along the western bank of the Ihuang

Shui, the 11th Army concentrated the 34th Division to the east of Linchuan, the Imai Detachment at Linchuan and the Ide Detachment in the vicinity of Sanchiangkou and made these three units responsible for the Army's rear flank and water routes.

Receiving a report on 9 June that the scattered Chinese 79th Army was gradually assembling its strength in the vicinity of Nancheng, the 3d Division and Takehara Detachment set out in pursuit of the enemy. On the 11th and 12th, these units annihilated enemy forces in the area and occupied Nancheng and its airfield.

On 10 June, the Iwanaga Detachment occupied Tengchiafou.

As the Chinese 100th Army had captured the Yingtanchen sector along the Chekiang-Kiangsi railway line, it stood in the way of the 11th Army's eastward advance along the line. The 11th Army, therefore, having attached the Iwanaga Detachment to the 34th Division, transferred the Division from Linchuan to the Chekiang-Kiangsi railway area in order that it might cooperate with the 13th Army's campaigns. At the same time, it ordered the Takehara Detachment to maintain Nancheng and the 3d Division to concentrate its strength near Chinchi by the 15th and await further orders.

On 15 and 16 June, the 34th Division, assisted by the air force, struck at the enemy between Yingtanchen and Kueichi and, on the 16th, captured Kueichi.

The Iwanaga Detachment continued to advance and on 1 July contacted the Yazu Detachment of the 13th Army at Hengfeng.

Temporary Occupation of Tracts along the Chekiang-Kiangsi Railway

In order to destroy and prevent the reconstruction of enemy airfields along the Chekiang-Kiangsi railway, and to transport captured materials, particularly railway material, to the rear area Imperial General Headquarters planned to occupy temporarily the region along the railway line.

At this time the 13th Army had only one railway battalion under its command. So that the captured materials might be transported to the rear area, therefore, Imperial General Headquarters transferred three railway battalions from the Kwantung Army to the 13th Army. These battalions arrived at Hangchou about the middle of June.

For the purpose of strengthening the garrison force, during the latter part of June, the Commander in Chief of the China Expeditionary Army reinforced the 13th Army with the Nara Detachment (two infantry battalions)[2] from the North China Area Army.

It was estimated that the period of occupation of the Chekiang-Kiangsi railway area for the purpose of transporting supplies to the

---

2. The basic manuscript shows three infantry battalions. The Commander in Chief of the China Expeditionary Army actually ordered three infantry battalions to be sent, but because of the tense situation in north China, the North China Area Army was able to send only two infantry battalions.

rear area would be approximately one month, however, bad weather and other factors extended the required period of occupation to two months.

Garrisoning and Offensive Operations by the 13th Army

As the territory occupied by the 13th Army increased, the task of supervising certain sectors was gradually placed under the command of the divisions. The Army began its occupation around 20 June and, subsequent to the capture of Shangjao, the following sectors along the Chekiang-Kiangsi railway were placed under the command of the designated divisions:

22d Division	Vicinity of Shangjao
32d Division	Vicinity of Yushan
15th Division	Vicinity of Kuangfeng
Kono Mixed Brigade	Vicinity of Chiangshan
116th Division	Vicinity of Chuhsien and Lungyu
70th Division	The Chekiang-Kiangsi railway north of and including the Chinhua-Lanchi sector.
Harada Mixed Brigade	Along the Fuchun Chiang After the withdrawal of the Fuchun Chiang Lines of Communication Unit on 12 July, the Brigade concentrated its strength at Lungyu.

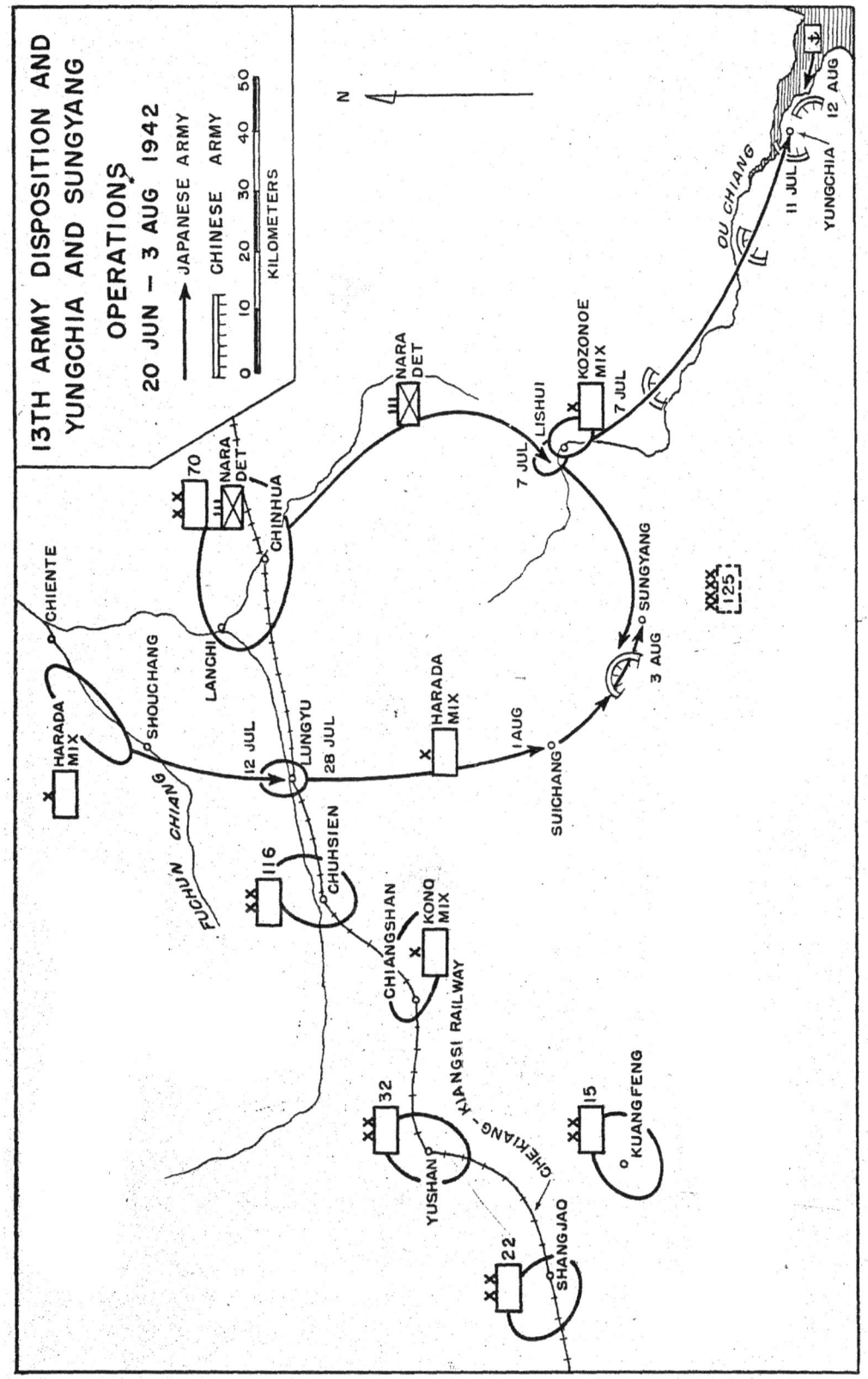

The Chinese apparently estimated that, as in the past, the Japanese forces would withdraw immediately after the offensive. They, therefore, conducted an offensive on the western front but were repulsed. On the other fronts and within the occupied area there were guerrilla attacks but no counterattacks on a large scale were undertaken. During this time the 13th Army successfully conducted the Yungchia and Sungyang Operations, destroyed airfields and other military installations and transported confiscated materials to the rear area. (Map 12)

Yungchia Operation

The objectives of this operation were to destroy the transportation routes by which Chinese junks, as well as British and American submarines, were smuggling supplies into the Chinese and also to destroy those bases at which these submarines were being refuelled and replenished by the Chinese.

On 2 July, the 13th Army ordered the Kozonoe Mixed Brigade at Lishui to proceed to the neighborhood of Yungchia and in order to protect the Brigade's rear, the 70th Division was ordered to maintain the area in the vicinity of Lishui.

On 7 July, the Brigade (minus one infantry battalion and one mountain artillery company) left Lishui and, destroying the enemy on the way, captured Yungchia on the 11th. At the same time the 70th Division disposed the main force of the Nara Detachment in the vicinity of Lishui.

On the 12th, after penetrating underwater obstacles (including small craft which had been sunk by the floods) the Navy landed and destroyed the enemy located in the sector below Yungchia. On the 16th, it began clearing the hazardous Ou Chiang for navigation and, by the 20th, the sea route to Yungchia had been cleared.

Sungyang Operation

This operation was conducted in order to defeat the enemy in the Sungyang area and to destroy the remaining enemy bases in Chekiang Province.

On 28 July, in accordance with 13th Army orders, the Harada Mixed Brigade (principally composed of four infantry battalions) left the Lungyu area and, on 1 August, captured Suichang. The Brigade, together with the recently attached Nara Detachment, then initiated a pincer movement to the west of Sungyang and, on 3 August, captured this sector.

In order that confiscated materials might be transported to the rear areas as expeditiously as possible the railways had to be repaired. Climatic conditions retarded the progress of this work but on 30 July the railways were finally ready for use.

Railway equipment located east of Yushan was the principal material confiscated and in order to transport this material to the area west of Chinhua, as planned, it was necessary to use the railways, vehicles and civilian vessels.

The destruction of airfields was assigned to the following divisions: Yushan airfield, 22d Division; Chuhsien airfield, 116th Division and Lishui airfield, 70th Division. Subsequent to the occupation of captured areas, the divisions began the destruction of the airfields and by the middle of August had completed this assignment.

11th Army's Operation in the Chekiang-Kiangsi Area

On 16 June the 11th Army captured the key position of Kueichi on the Chekiang-Kiangsi railway line and ordered the 34th Division to defend the area along the railway. In order to prepare for any counterattacks the Army deployed the 3d Division in the vicinity of Wuwan, the Takehara Detachment in the Nancheng area, the Imai Detachment in the neighborhood of Linchuan and the Ide Detachment near Sanchiangkou. (Map 13)

Prior to this, the Hirano Detachment, in cooperation with the Navy, made an assault near Tuchang and, on 15 June, landed at the mouth of the Hsin Ho. The Detachment then sailed up the Hsin Ho and maintained the water route in the lower reaches of the river near Kueichi. This water route and the Fu Ho water route played an important role in the transportation of material during the occupation.

With the failure of the 79th Army to occupy Linchuan, Pi Yueh, commander of the 9th War Sector Army, placed the 58th Army (two divisions) under the command of the 4th Army (3 divisions) which during the latter part of May had moved eastward from Changsha to Liuyang. At the same time, he issued strict orders to recapture Linchuan. During the latter part of June the 58th Army captured the line of heights on the left bank of the Fu Ho, west of Linchuan and the 4th Army, passing along the east bank of the Ihuang Shui, gradually moved in on Linchuan. The 11th Army waited for an opportunity to counter this enemy thrust. The 4th Army began to shift into defensive positions along the Linchuan-Wuwan sector and, taking advantage of this, the 11th Army decided to destroy the enemy. The attack opened on the night of 25 June.

The Takehara Detachment spearheaded the thrust toward Chungjen and cut the enemy escape route. The 3d Division, after seizing the main force of the 4th Army along the banks of the Ihuang Shui, advanced toward Chungjen, while the Imai Detachment advanced along the Ihuang Shui to Ihuang. It then disposed its strength in this sector in order to cut the enemy's escape routes.

The 11th Army concentrated its siege to the region between Ihuang and Lichi and, by the 30th, had annihilated the main strength of the Chinese 4th Army.

During this operation the Chinese 58th Army had been ordered to attack the flanks of the 11th Army, but, on the night of 30 June, the 58th Army withdrew to a line running from north to south of Hsiutsai-

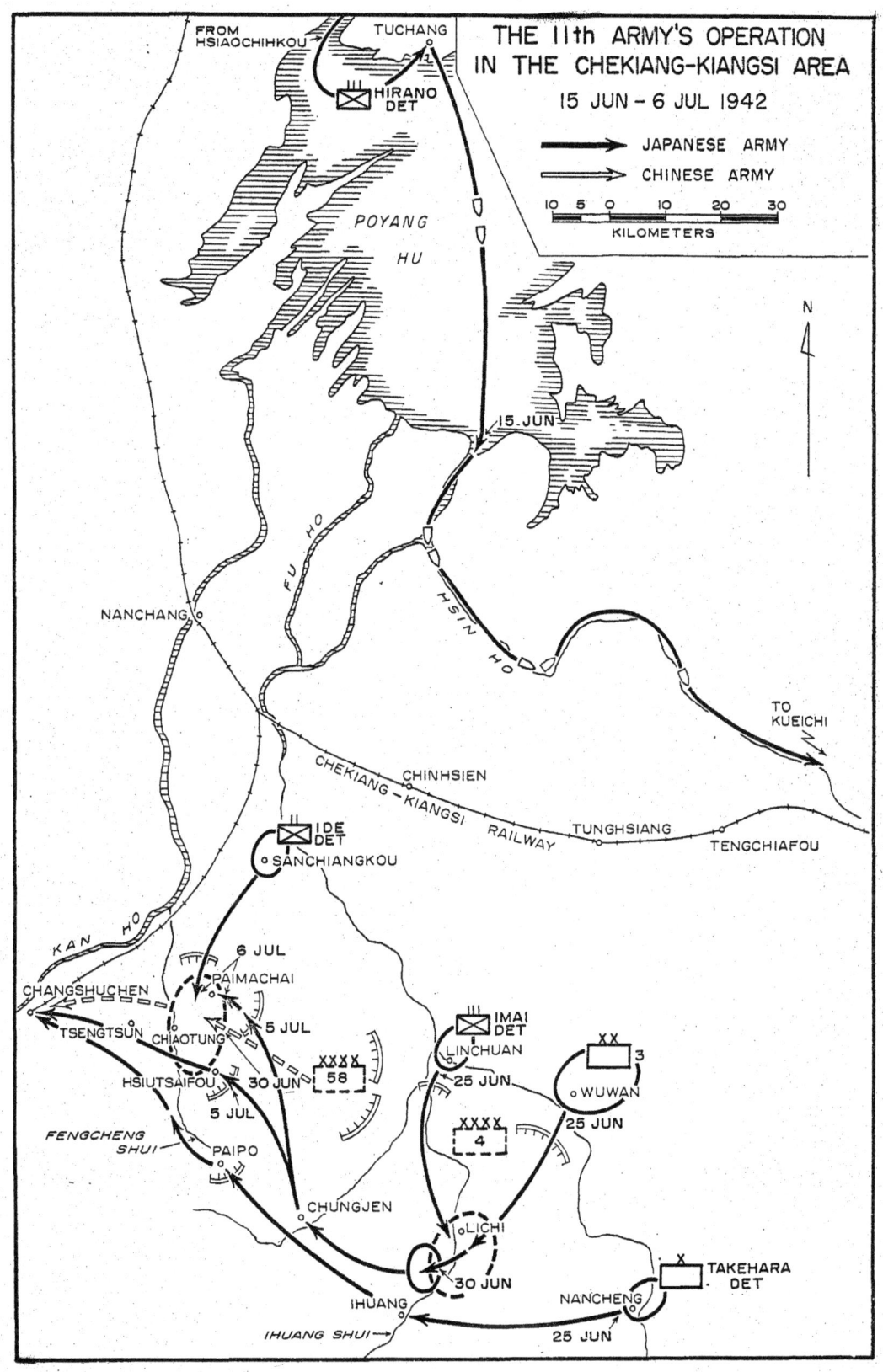

fou.

Having adjusted its fighting strength along the Ihuang Shui, the 11th Army decided to use the 3d Division and the Takehara Detachment to destroy the 58th Army which was then retreating from the Chungjen area. The 3d Division was ordered to attack the enemy at Paimachai and Hsiutsaifou. The Takehara Detachment, after destroying the enemy in the Paipo area, was to advance through the Fengcheng Shui valley into the Tsengtsun sector. Part of the Detachment was to thrust toward Changshuchen and cut the enemy's escape routes.

The attacking units began their offensive as planned. The enemy in the Hsiutsaifou area stoutly resisted until their rear units finally began to retreat to the Changshuchen area. The 11th Army immediately dispatched units from the Takehara Detachment and the 3d Division to Changshuchen. The Ide Detachment also participated in this engagement. By the evening of 6 July, the 11th Army had annihilated the main force of the 58th Army in the area east of Chiaotung, and the defeated enemy fled to the distant mountains.

During the early part of July, the Imai Detachment destroyed the Nancheng Airfield.

About mid-July, the 11th Army ordered the return of the main force of the 3d Division and the Imai and Takehara Detachments to their original stations, when the 3d Division was to be reorganized.

The remaining units (composed mainly of 15 infantry battalions and 7 mountain artillery battalions) were ordered to maintain the line from the vicinity of Wuwan along the lower reaches of the Fu Ho, the region along the Chekiang-Kiangsi railway west of Kueichi and the Hsin Ho. These units were also ordered to cooperate with the 13th Army. Upon its return, the Takehara Detachment took up positions in the neighborhood of Nanchang as an Army reserve unit.

Estimating that the partial withdrawal of Japanese forces meant a withdrawal on all fronts, the enemy shifted the 35th Army (which had been facing the 13th Army) and other units to the 11th Army front, and in the latter part of July, became active along this front.

To facilitate future withdrawals, during the early part of August, the 11th Army mopped up the enemy in the surrounding districts, especially in the Tunghsiang-Wuwan sector.

Reverse Operation

On 28 July, Imperial General Headquarter ordered the Commander in Chief of the China Expeditionary Army to maintain key points in the Chinhua sector after the termination of the campaign in Chekiang Province. The order read that the withdrawal would take place around 20 August but that a force would remain to maintain those important regions in the vicinity of Chinhua from which such raw materials as fluorite, copper and tin were obtained. Consideration was also to be given to the conservation of manpower.

Reverse Movement of the 13th Army

Complying with this order, the Commander in Chief of the China Expeditionary Army set the date for the commencement of the withdrawal as 19 August and ordered the 13th Army to provide approximately one division for the occupation of the Chinhua area. The occupation zone was to cover an area from Fuchuan Chiang in the west to a line from Lanchi to Chinhua, Wui, Hsinchang and Fenghua in the east.

The 13th Army withdrawal was divided into two phases. In the first phase, the units west of Chuhsien were to be concentrated in the neighborhood of Chuhsien and, in the second phase, these units were to shift their concentration from Chuhsien to Chinhua. The responsibility for the Chinhua region was entrusted to the 22d Division and that for Hangchou, Ningpo and Chenghsien regions to the 70th Division.

For the first phase of the withdrawal, the 13th Army issued the following orders to its units west of Chuhsien:

> In order to establish a position at Lishui when the main force of the Army concentrates at Chuhsien, on 15 August the Kozonoe Mixed Brigade will withdraw from Yungchia toward Lishui.
> The Kono Mixed Brigade will move south to Shihmenshih to facilitate the withdrawal of the 15th Division.
> The 22d and 15th Divisions and the Kono Mixed Brigade will withdraw in parallel lines, being prepared at all times for

counterattacks.
> The 32d Division will withdraw prior to the withdrawal of the 22d Division, by way of the latter's route of advance.

Between 24 and 25 August, the units assembled without mishap in the vicinity of Chuhsien.

The plan for the second phase of the withdrawal was that the 32d Division, which was to effect its withdrawal first, and the 22d Division, which was responsible for the occupation of the Chinhua region, would begin to withdraw at the same time toward the Chinhua area. The 116th and 15th Divisions, together with the Kono, Harada and Kozonoe Mixed Brigades would make a parallel withdrawal.

On 26 August, the 32d and 22d Divisions began their withdrawal and, by the 29th, their strength was concentrated in the Chinhua region along both banks of the Chu Chiang. The other units began their withdrawal on 27 August and had assembled in the Chinhua-Lanchi sector between 30 and 31 August.

While occupying the Chinhua region, the 22d Division was entrusted with the additional task of defending the Iwu-Wui area where large quantities of mineral resources existed.

By mid-September, the 22d Division had, in general, completed its fortifications. The lines of fortifications in the occupied territory and the boundary lines between the 22d Division and the 70th Division are shown on Map 14.

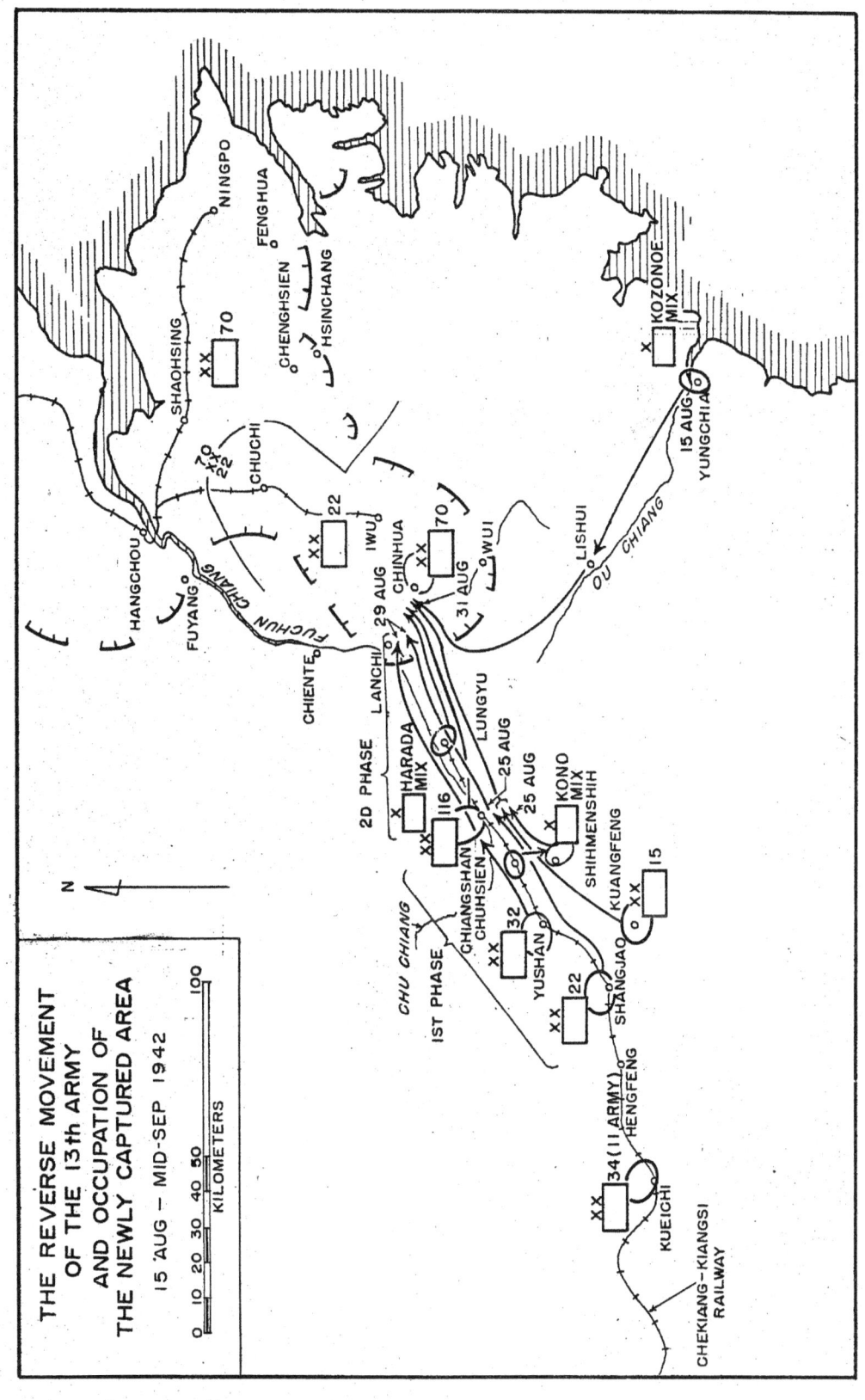

Reverse Movement of the 11th Army

In accordance with orders from the China Expeditionary Army, the 11th Army gradually withdrew its forces from the first line without interference from the enemy. By 27 August, the Army had concentrated its main forces near Nanchang.

Casualties During Reverse Operation

The casualties sustained during this operation were:

	13th Army	11th Army	Total
Dead	1,284	356	1,640
Wounded	2,767	949	3,716
Sick	11,812	unknown	
Horses Killed	2,311	240	2,561
Sick Horses	2,411	unknown	
Wounded Horses	462	100	562

Plan to Capture Szechwan Province

As the operations in the south had progressed satisfactorily and by spring of 1942 the objective areas had, for the most part, been occupied, Imperial General Headquarters decided to investigate the possibility of taking advantage of the favorable situation.

The large bases for supplies and reorganization of fighting strength as well as approximately one-half of the enemy's war production enterprises were located in Szechwan Province. This area was also known to be used as a pool for American air force strength.

It was estimated, therefore, that if the Japanese forces could deal a heavy blow to the Chinese Central Army which guarded this area and, at the same time, destroy the Chungking Government's bases of resistance, the possibility of defeating the enemy would be great. If this operation were successful, even though the enemy might not surrender, their position would be only that of a local government and the chances of promoting a settlement of the China Incident would be greatly improved. Furthermore, by occupying this area, any attempt by the British or American air forces to raid the Homeland from bases in China could be frustrated.

Imperial General Headquarters regarded this as an important objective both because it could bring about the submission of the Chungking Government and also because it could help to expand the success of the initial phase of the Pacific War. An immediate decision, however, could not be made due to the changing conditions both in Japan and abroad as well as to the indefinite national strength. Preparations were ordered which would not affect other areas to any great extent as it was considered necessary to use every opportunity to conduct operations against China when the overall situation permitted.

The plan required the annihilation of the main force of the Chinese Central Army, the capture of key sectors in Szechwan Province, the destruction of enemy bases of resistance and the acceleration of the submission and capitulation of the Chungking Government. To attain these objectives, the main force of the China Expeditionary Army from the Changan area and an element from the Ichang area were to advance toward the Szechwan Plains. During this period, the already occupied territories were to be maintained and secured with the minimum strength necessary. Close unity was to be emphasized between the operational directives and the political and propaganda measures to be taken against Chungking.

It was planned that an Area Army from south Shansi Province with approximately ten divisions and an Army from Ichang area, with approximately six divisions, would commence their attacks in the spring of 1943. The Area Army, after securing the Changan area, was to advance to the vicinity of Kuangyuan and the Army was to advance into the area along a line running north and south of Wanhsien. With the completion of preparations in these areas, the offensive was to be taken. Chungking and Chengtu were to be occupied as well as the key sectors in Szechwan Province. If necessary, campaigns were then to be conducted to annihilate the enemy bases of resistance in essential areas.

The period for this operation was estimated to be approximately five months. During this time the occupied areas were to be maintained and secured and the enemy checked in order to facilitate the offensive operation.

The strength to be employed in this operation was the China Expeditionary Army to which were to be attached elements from the Homeland, Manchuria and the southern area.

On 3 September 1942, Imperial General Headquarters ordered the China Expeditionary Army to make the necessary preparations. During the latter part of September, however, due to the gradual shift in power in the Solomons Campaign, Imperial General Headquarters decided to postpone temporarily the dispatch of materiel required in the Szechwan Operation and gave orders to the China Expeditionary Army to this effect.

Toward the end of 1942, because of the adverse situation in the southeastern area and also because of lack of shipping, Imperial General Headquarters ordered the suspension of the Szechwan Operation. Further, it was decided that it would be impossible to conduct this operation in 1943. In fact, it was regarded as impossible to conduct active operations in the China area before the war situation in the southeastern Pacific improved considerably. Future operations in the China area were, therefore, to be conducted according to the following plan:

> The over-all situation of the Japanese Army is such that not only will the supply of men and materiel to China be stopped but divisions and other units will be sent from China to the south Pacific area and other points. Operations in China will be conducted according to the present mission of the China Expeditionary Army within the bounds mentioned above. Special emphasis will be placed upon

the necessity to maintain order in the occupied regions. Every effort will be made to conserve the fighting strength of the China Expeditionary Army until such time as the war situation in the south Pacific area is settled satisfactorily.

Aerial operations will be carried out in accordance with the changes in situation, especially to cope with the increase in the enemy air force. For the time being, however, operations will be limited to the present scale. Aerial warfare against China will be emphasized subsequent to the spring of next year and preparations will be undertaken for these increased aerial operations in order to crush the enemy's aerial initiative after the spring of 1943.

At the end of February 1943, the Commander in Chief of the China Expeditionary Army was given the following mission:

Occupied areas will be maintained. The enemy will be crushed and his will to continue the war destroyed.

Control of the air will be wrested from the enemy air force which is based in China. In spring the air force will be reinforced and aerial operations will be conducted in cooperation with a ground offensive.

Security will be maintained in cities as well as in areas with important natural resources and along lines of communication. Troops will be concentrated gradually in order to meet any change in the situation and the fighting strength will be increased.[3]

Transfer and Reorganization of China Expeditionary Army Forces

With the deterioration of the situation in the Southern Area,

---

3. In the original Japanese order the word "Chian" meaning peace and order, was avoided so that there might be no misunderstanding in regard to the duties of the Army. "Chian" might have

troops were gradually transferred there from the China Expeditionary Army and, by the summer of 1943, five divisions together with various other small units had been transferred. Through the autumn and winter of 1942, the 6th Division of the 11th Army, the 51st Division of the 23d Army and the 41st Division of the 1st Army were sent to the Southeastern Area while the 36th Division of the 1st Army was sent to the Southwestern Area. Toward the spring of 1943, the 15th Division of the 13th Army was transferred to the Burma Theater and the 17th Division, under the direct command of the China Expeditionary Army, was sent to the Southeastern Area.

In order to replenish the strength in the China Theater, four divisions were reorganized from independent mixed brigades, two independent mixed brigades were activated in China and, in May 1943, one division was sent from Japan. These units upon arrival were placed under the command of the China Expeditionary Army and assigned as follows:

---

3. (Cont'd) implied that the position of the Army over the occupied areas was in some sense political. At the same time, instructions were issued to give every incentive to the activities of the Wang Government.

Army	Units Assigned	Date of Orders	Remarks
Directly attached to the North China Area Army	63d Div	1 May 42	Reorganized from the 15th Indep Brig
1st Army	62d Div	1 May 42	Reorganized from the 4th and 6th Indep Brigs
11th Army	17th Indep Mixed Brig	17 Dec 42	From the 13th Army
13th Army	61st Div	16 May 43	Activated in the Japan
13th Army	64th Div	1 May 43	Reorganized from the 12th Indep Brig
13th Army	65th Div	1 May 43	Reorganized from the 13th Indep Brig
23d Army	22d Indep Mixed Brig	27 Nov 42	
23d Army	23d Indep Mixed Brig	8 Jan 43	

It was impossible to send sufficient air strength to China. In the spring of 1943, the total air strength in China was six regiments (two fighter regiments, one attack regiment, one reconnaissance regiment and two light bomber regiments) one independent reconnaissance squadron and various ground service units.

CHAPTER 4

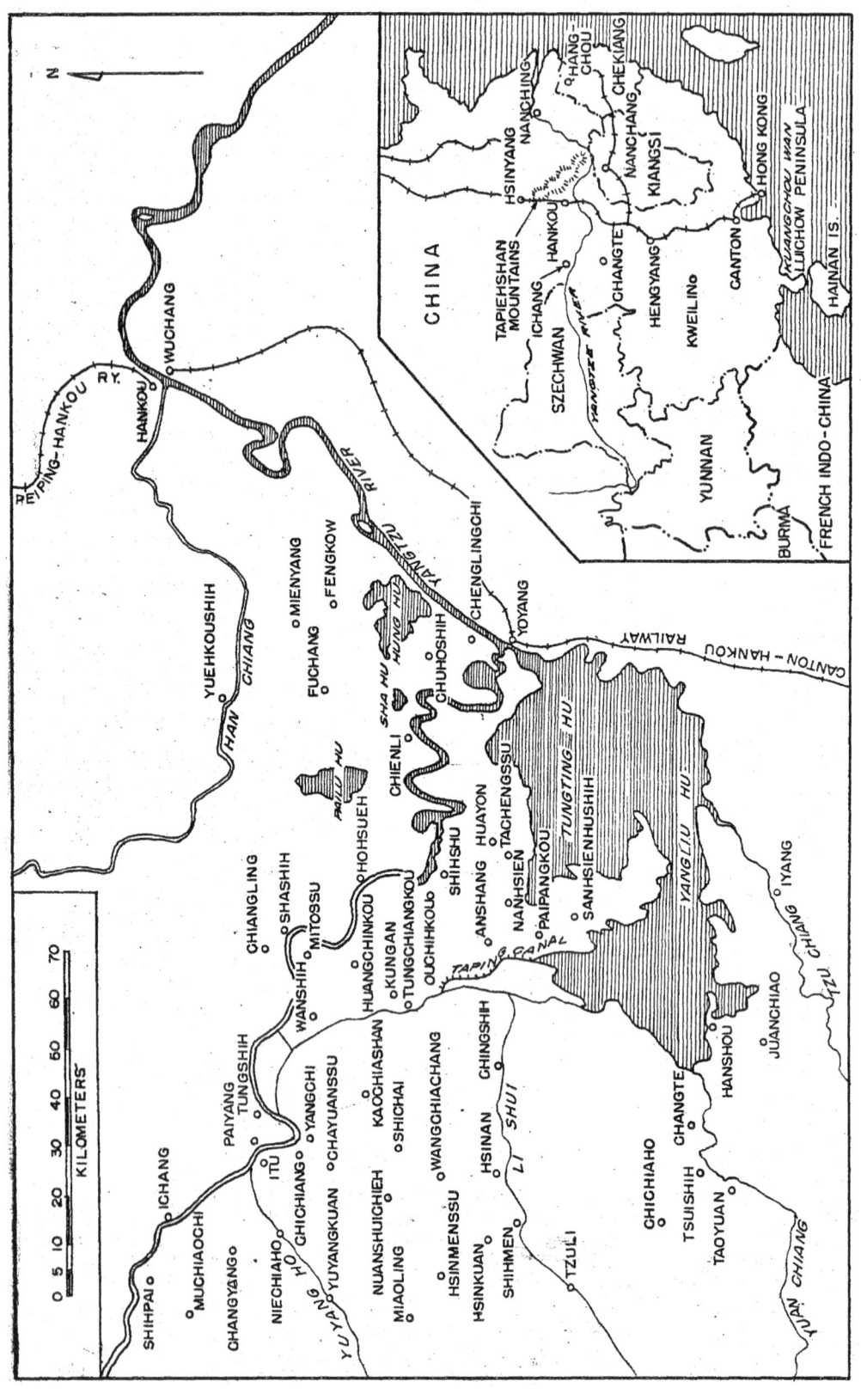

CHAPTER 4

Operations in 1943

Luichow Peninsula Operation and the Occupation of Kuangchou Wan

About January 1943, the enemy began to show great interest in and dispatched powerful espionage groups to the Kuangchou Wan area. Further, they had concentrated two divisions as units ready to be deployed in the region to the west of Canton and were in the process of withdrawing one or two armies from the Ichang area. It was impossible, from this information, to anticipate whether immediate capture of Kuangchou Wan was planned but, fearing that the enemy might seize the initiative as a result of a possible break in diplomatic relations between the Chungking Government and France, Imperial General Headquarters on 31 January ordered the China Expeditionary Army in cooperation with the Navy, to capture the important sectors of the Luichow Peninsula as soon as possible and to advance to Kuangchow Wan.

Imperial General Headquarters also issued the Army-Navy Agreement, an outline of which follows:

Outline of Operation:

> The Army, in cooperation with the Navy, will make a surprise landing on the eastern shores of the Luichow Peninsula and capture the key points on the peninsula. Prepations will then be made to advance to Kuangchou Wan.

The assault upon Luichow Peninsula will be made about mid-February. Details will be worked out jointly by the Commander in Chief of the China Expeditionary Army and the China Area Fleet commander.

Advance into Kuangchou Wan will be by separate order and, if possible, will be conducted in a friendly manner.

After advancing into Kuangchou Wan, the Army will cooperate with the French in maintaining peace and order. Key sectors along the Luichow Peninsula will be occupied.

Should the Chungking Army infiltrate prior to the Army's advance or should the French refuse to cooperate and resist, the Army will destroy these obstacles and take Kuangchou Wan.

Strength to be Employed:

Army: Three infantry battalions under the command of the commander of the 23d Army.
Part of the Air Force Unit.

Navy: Fixed strength of the China Area Fleet Commander subordinate to the 2d China Expeditionary Fleet Commander.

Progress of Operation

Complying with orders from Imperial General Headquarters, the China Expeditionary Army ordered the commander of the 23d Army to order a unit composed of three infantry battalions of the 23d Independent Mixed Brigade[1] to execute this operation.

---

1. One battalion of the Brigade remained in Hong Kong.

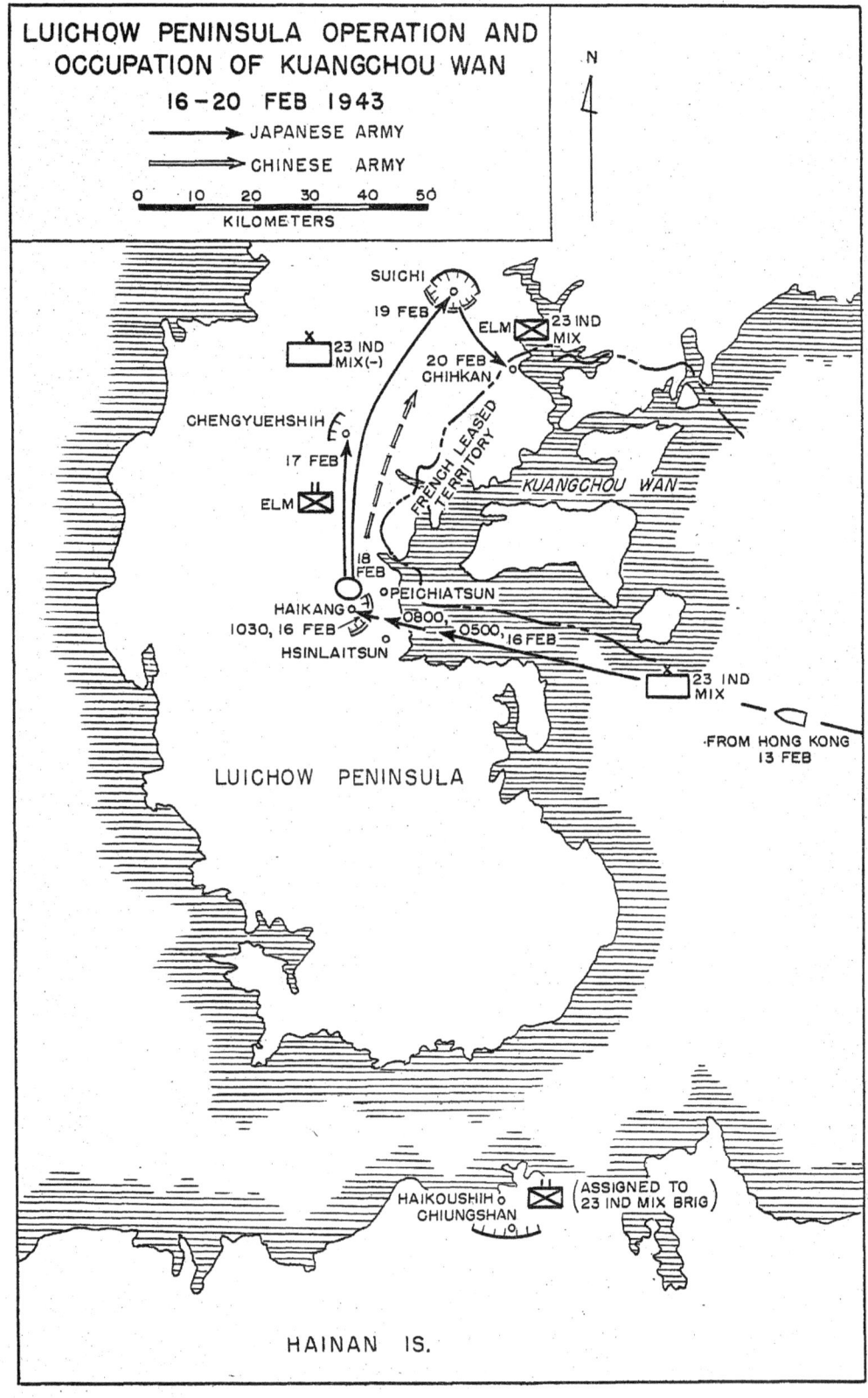

On 13 February, the 23d Independent Mixed Brigade left Hong Kong and at 0500 on the 16th, the first wave (Brigade headquarters, two infantry battalions, part of the artillery and the major part of the engineer and signal corps) in coordination with the naval and air units made a surprise landing. The force made its way through 1500 meters of knee-deep shoals, and by 0800 of the same day had advanced to the Peichiatsun-Hsinlaitsun line. At 1030 it had captured Haikang. About this time, part of the Chinese 4th Garrison Group, which had been defending this area, retreated toward Suichi. (Map 15)

On 17 February, a unit (composed mainly of one infantry battalion and the main force of the engineer unit) was ordered to advance to Chengyuehshih, 27 km north of Haikang. On the 18th, the main force of the Brigade left Haikang and on the 19th arrived at Suichi.

As a result of negotiations with the French authorities, on 20 February, a local agreement was reached whereby part of the Japanese force advanced into the French leased territory.

The 23d Army placed one infantry battalion on Hainan Island under the command of the commander of the 23d Independent Mixed Brigade and assigned to the commander the task of defending the northern part of Hainan Island in addition to defending the key sectors of Luichow Peninsula.[2]

Kuangte Operation

During the offensive warfare against Nanching in 1937, the Japanese forces temporarily occupied the Kuangte area. The enemy persistently counterattacked and feeling that it was impossible to maintain the area due to lack of transportation facilities, the Japanese forces withdrew.[3] For the purpose of economizing on manpower and strengthening the Wuchang-Hankou area during the Wuchang-Hankou Operation in 1938, Japanese troops were disposed from the vicinity of Hsuancheng to Wanchihchen. Hsuancheng and Kuangte were beyond the limits of this zone of occupation and readily became key bases for enemy counterattacks.[4]

Again in 1940, during the operation in the area south of the Yangtze River, Japanese forces occupied the sector in the vicinity of Hsuancheng and Kuangte but again, due to lack of troop strength, the Japanese forces withdrew.[5] Enemy guerrillas were quick to take advantage of these withdrawals and to use the area as a base from which to harass the Japanese Army.

---

2. As the official records of this operation were destroyed, the details described above were compiled from telegrams located in the files of the 1st Demobilization Bureau.
3. Monograph No 179, *Central China Area Operations Record, 1937-1941*.
4. *Ibid*.
5. *Ibid*.

MAP NO. 16

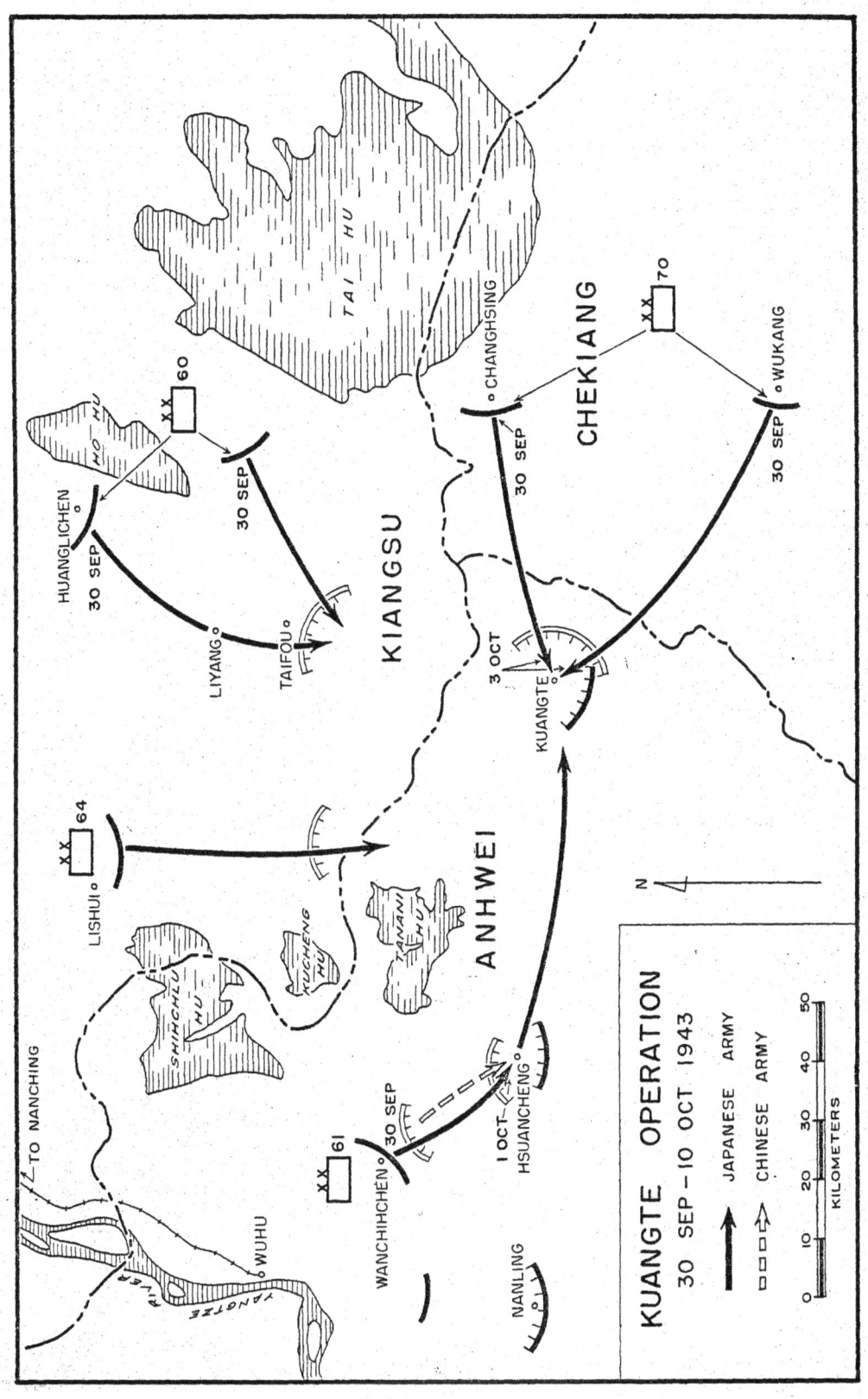

About August 1943, the Nanching Government, supported by the China Expeditionary Army, successfully executed the "Seigo-Kosaku Operation" (country-clearing operation) in order to mop up the guerrillas and communist forces in the area. As a result, the 13th Army was able to assemble a strong mobile force to undertake the Kuangte Operation at the end of September. The four divisions to be employed were deployed as follows:

The 61st Division was ordered to assemble at Wanchihchen for an attack on Hsuancheng; the 64th Division was to attack Hsuancheng from the region east of Kucheng Hu and Tanani Hu; the 60th Division was ordered to assemble to the west of Tai Hu and to attack Liyang and the area to the south; while the 70th Division was to attack Kuangte and the surrounding area from Changhsing and Wukang. (Map 16)

Attacks were opened on 30 September and the enemy began to retreat. On 1 October, the 61st Division captured Hsuancheng with little resistance from the enemy. Subsequently, it advanced to the Kuangte area. On 3 October, the 70th Division occupied Kuangte.

The 64th Division's attack was delayed due to the difficulty it experienced in crossing the Yangtze River but the 60th Division proceeded as planned and defeated the enemy in the mountain area to the south of Taifou.

The operation closed on 10 October. The Nanling-Hsuancheng-Kuangte line was designated the main line of resistance and security units were dispatched there. The boundary line between Anhwei and Kiangsu Provinces was specified as the line dividing the regions to be secured by the 61st and 60th Divisions respectively.[6]

Operation North of the Yangtze River

The mission of the 11th Army was to occupy important regions with the Wuchang-Hankou sector as a focal point encircled by Nanchang, Hsiaochihkou, Yoyang, Ichang and Hsinyang and to destroy the enemy's fighting strength. The Chinese still occupied the triangle zone on the northern side of the Yangtze River with Mienyang as its central point. This region wedged into the Wuchang-Hankou area like a dagger and the enemy took full advantage of its strategic position. It was therefore planned to extend the Japanese occupational zone in order to strengthen its position and destroy the enemy in the area.

The 11th Army had previously undertaken two or three reconnaissance operations in force but, hampered by the difficult terrain and strong enemy fortifications, had failed to wipe out the enemy.

The enemy force in this area was the reorganized irregular

---

6. There are no official records of this operation available. Details given above were written mainly from information supplied from memory by Lt Col Kenji Shindo, at that time a staff officer of the 13th Army.

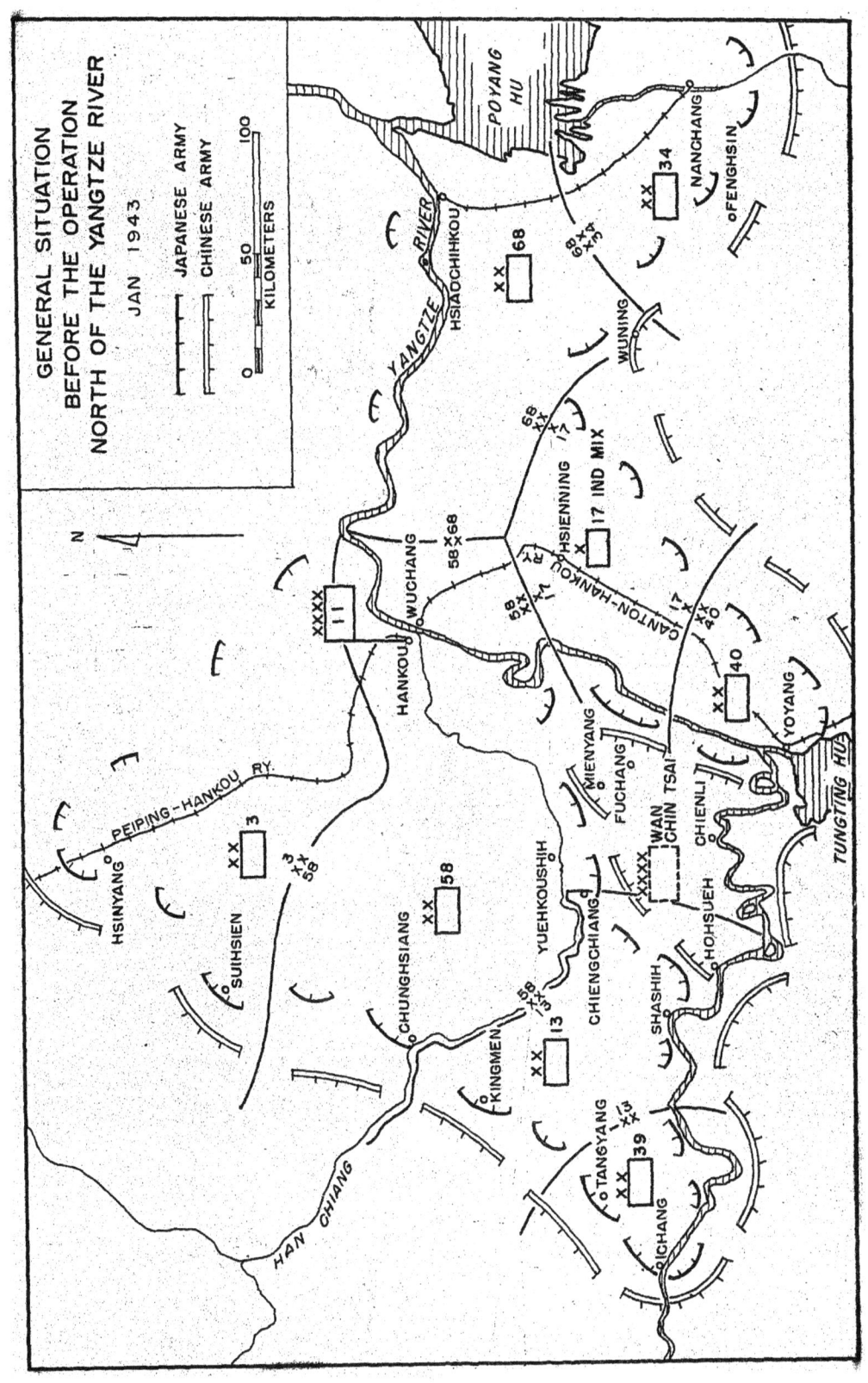

Communist Army which had existed in the Kiangsi Province around 1931 and 1932. When the Communist Army made a mass movement to the northwest, this reorganized army had settled in the triangle region. It was an independent unit, isolated from and unfriendly to the Nationalist Army. In fact, these two forces often clashed with each other. In its organization, drills, tactics and treatment of the population it showed very definite characteristics of the Communist Army. Its arms and ammunitions were self-manufactured and although adequate in quantity were inferior in quality. The strength of this force was estimated to be approximately nine independent brigades (one brigade had a total strength of from 6,000 to 8,000 men) with Wang Chin-Tsai as the commander. In order to secure their independent status they had dispersed their fortifications and taken every advantage of the terrain.

In November 1942, the 6th Division was withdrawn from the 11th Army and, in December, the 17th Independent Mixed Brigade was transferred to the Army. The disposition of the 11th Army, as well as that of enemy forces north of the Yangtze River, in January 1943 were as shown on Map 17.

From the end of May until August 1942, the 11th Army had carried out the Chekiang-Kiangsi Operation and from mid-December until mid-January 1943, using the 3d Division as its main force, had mopped up the enemy in the vicinity of Mt Tapiehshan. Then, without time to regroup and reorganize its forces, at the beginning of February the Army was ordered to commence the operation north of the Yangtze River.

Operational Command

In former operations against the enemy in the triangle region along the northern shore of the Tungting Hu attacks had been directed from the north against the enemy's front but, due to the enemy's impregnable fortifications, these attacks had proved unsuccessful.

It was planned, therefore, that this operation would be a surprise attack on the enemy's rear. Further, sufficient strength was to be trained to conduct attacks against enemy emplacements.

Operational Plan:

The strength to be employed during the operation is:

11th Army Headquarters

13th Division (approximately 6 infantry battalions and 3 mountain artillery battalions)

40th Division (approximately 6 infantry battalions and 2 mountain artillery battalions)

58th Division (approximately 4 infantry battalions and 2 artillery battalions)

Necessary units under the direct command of the Army (the Army will be reinforced with engineer and shipping engineer units)

44th Air Regiment (direct cooperation)

The 13th and 40th Divisions will concentrate their strength in the Shashih and Yoyang areas respectively. Measures will be taken to deceive the enemy into believing that these concentrations will have a direct bearing on preparations for the offensive operation against the Changsha area. Movement of the 58th Division will be kept secret. With the progress of the battle situation, however, the strength of the 58th Division will gradually concentrate at the southern main line of resistance of the present line of occupation.

The operation will be divided into two phases. In the first phase, the enemy in the area immediately north of the Yangtze River will be defeated. In the second phase, enemy bases in the Mienyang and Fengkow areas will be destroyed. After the conclusion of this operation the triangle region will be divided into three distinct sectors with the Pailu Hu as the central point. Defense of these sectors will be allotted to the 58th, 13th and 40th Divisions.

Progress of Operations

From the early part of February the 13th and 40th Divisions initiated their unit concentrations and by mid-February had completed their concentrations according to plan. At that time the 58th Division refrained from any sort of troop movement.

On 15 February, the 40th Division surreptitiously crossed the Yangtze River and moved toward the enemy bases in the Chuhoshih area. An element of the Division annihilated the enemy forces south of Sha Hu and around Chienli. (Map 18)

On the same day, using its main force from the western district of Pailu Hu and an element from the area east of the lake, the 13th Division attacked enemy bases in the region south of Pailu Hu.

The enemy was taken entirely by surprise and withdrew from its prepared positions. While part of this force was annihilated some elements escaped by the Yangtze River and others fled toward Mienyang, where the main Chinese force was in position.

The second phase of the operation was opened on 21 February.

In order to accomplish the destruction of the enemy bases at Mienyang, Fengkow and Fuchang in the triangle region, the Army ordered the 58th Division to constrict its line of seige in the north according to the progress of the battle situation. At the same time the 13th and 40th Divisions were directed to conduct their attacks from the region east of Pailu Hu and both sides of the Hung Hu respectively.

Each division went into action and enemy bases in the area were destroyed. After an intensive search and pursuit action, Wang Chin-Tsai, the enemy commander, was captured by the cavalry regiment of the 40th Division. The reconnaissance and bombing conducted by the 44th Air Regiment were especially effective and greatly contributed toward the destruction of the enemy.

Apart from the annihilation of the major part of the enemy force, approximately 4,000 to 5,000 men under the command of Chin

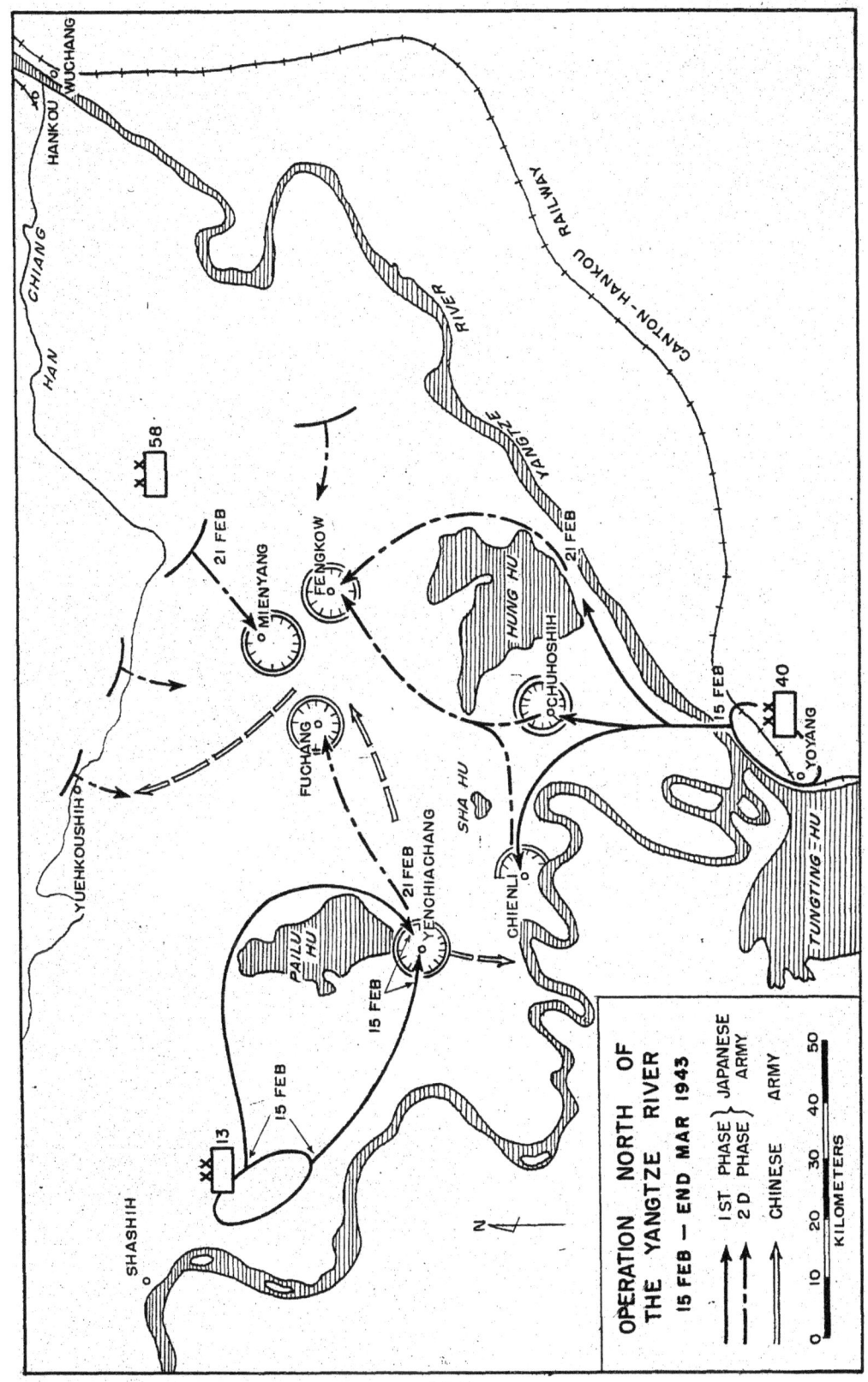

I-wu and Su Chen-Tung surrendered to the 58th Division at Yuehkoushih. However, part of the enemy force escaped by passing through the lines as native civilians.

The operation was concluded at the end of March.

The triangle region was divided into three sectors and the 58th, 40th and 13th Divisions were made responsible for their respective allotted sectors. The main line of resistance of defense was advanced to the Yangtze River.

Casualties sustained by the Japanese Army during this operation were:

    Dead   354
    Wounded   890
    Horses killed 69
    Horses wounded 56

As a result of this operation, not only did the Japanese Army obtain a fertile region and suppress the enemy in the Wuchang-Hankou area but it placed the Army in a favorable position in regard to future operations against the area along the western shore of the Tungting Hu.[6]

---

6. As there were no official documents available in regard to this operation, details were written from information supplied from memory by Sentaro Azuma, a staff officer of the 11th Army at the time of the operation.

Operation South of the Yangtze River

Situation Prior to the Operation

After the outbreak of the Pacific War, due mainly to the activity of enemy submarines, Japanese shipping losses gradually increased. With the deterioration of the situation in that area, there was an increased demand for shipping to be used in the transporting of men and munitions and also the necessary raw materials for the production of munitions in Japan. As a result there was no shipping available to be allotted to the China Theater although river shipping in the interior of China decreased yearly. Around Ichang there was approximately 20,000 tons of steamer tonnage for inland river navigation. It was felt, therefore, that if this shipping could be captured and used to supplement the shipping tonnage in the China Theater, it would greatly alleviate the position. For this purpose it was necessary to occupy the right bank of the Yangtze River between Ichang and Yoyang. The China Expeditionary Army, therefore, planned to advance in May 1943 to the southern bank of the Yangtze River in order to open the river for navigation and to crush the enemy's fighting strength located there.

As a result of the operation to the north of the Yangtze River in February and March 1943, Japanese forces occupied the Yangtze River bank from Shashih to Yoyang. At the same time, an element occupied the Shihshu area on the right bank of the river. In order to facilitate the present operation, between 9 to 15 April, the 40th Division advanced to the neighborhood of Huayon and captured the line running east and west of this town.

The Army planned to destroy the enemy around Anshang and Nanhsien with a powerful force composed mainly of the 3d Division, the 17th Independent Mixed Brigade, the Koshiba Detachment (three battalions of the 40th Division), and the Harigaya Detachment (three battalions from the 34th Division) and subsequently to attack both flanks of the enemy between Chichiang and Kungan from the north with the 3d Division, the 13th Division and the Nozoe Detachment (three battalions from the 58th Division). The 39th, 3d and 13th Divisions, deployed parallel to each other, were to defeat the enemy northwest of Ichang.

The Army ordered the 3d Division and the 17th Independent Mixed Brigade to concentrate their strength in the area around Shihshu, the Toda Detachment at Huayon, the Koshiba Detachment between Shihshu and Huayon and the Harigaya Detachment at Chenglingchi. It also directed the 13th Division to concentrate its strength in the vicinity of Paiyang and Tungshih by 10 May and the 39th Division to assemble in the Ichang area by 18 May.

Concentrations were begun on 16 April and concluded on 4 May.

Progress of Operation (Map 19)

First Phase:

In order to annihilate the enemy at Anshang and Nanhsien, the 11th Army directed the 3d Division to attack the enemy at Anshang and in the area to the west; the 17th Independent Mixed Brigade to attack Anshang and the area to the east; the Koshiba Detachment to attack in the Nanhsien region; the Toda Detachment to penetrate Tachengssu and attack the enemy in the Sanhsienhushih area while the Harigaya Detachment was to advance by water through Tungting Hu and Yangliu Hu, land near Paipangkou and Sanhsienhushih and attack the enemy there.

On 5 May the units opened their attacks. The 3d Division attacked the enemy west of Ouchihkou and advanced southward along the western banks of the Taping Canal; the 17th Independent Mixed Brigade, in coordination with the 3d Division, broke through enemy positions southwest of Ouchihkou and advanced southward; the Koshiba Detachment advanced southward from the area south of Ouchihkou; the Toda Detachment attacked Tachengssu from the region east of Huayon;, while the Harigaya Detachment crossed Tungting Hu, destroyed enemy positions and obstacles near Yangliu Hu and advanced to the area south of Nanhsien.

At the beginning of the operation, the main force of the 44th Air Regiment cooperated with the Harigaya Detachment and later coordinated with the offensive actions of the various other units. Subsequently, the 3d Division defeated the enemy moving toward the

MAP NO. 19

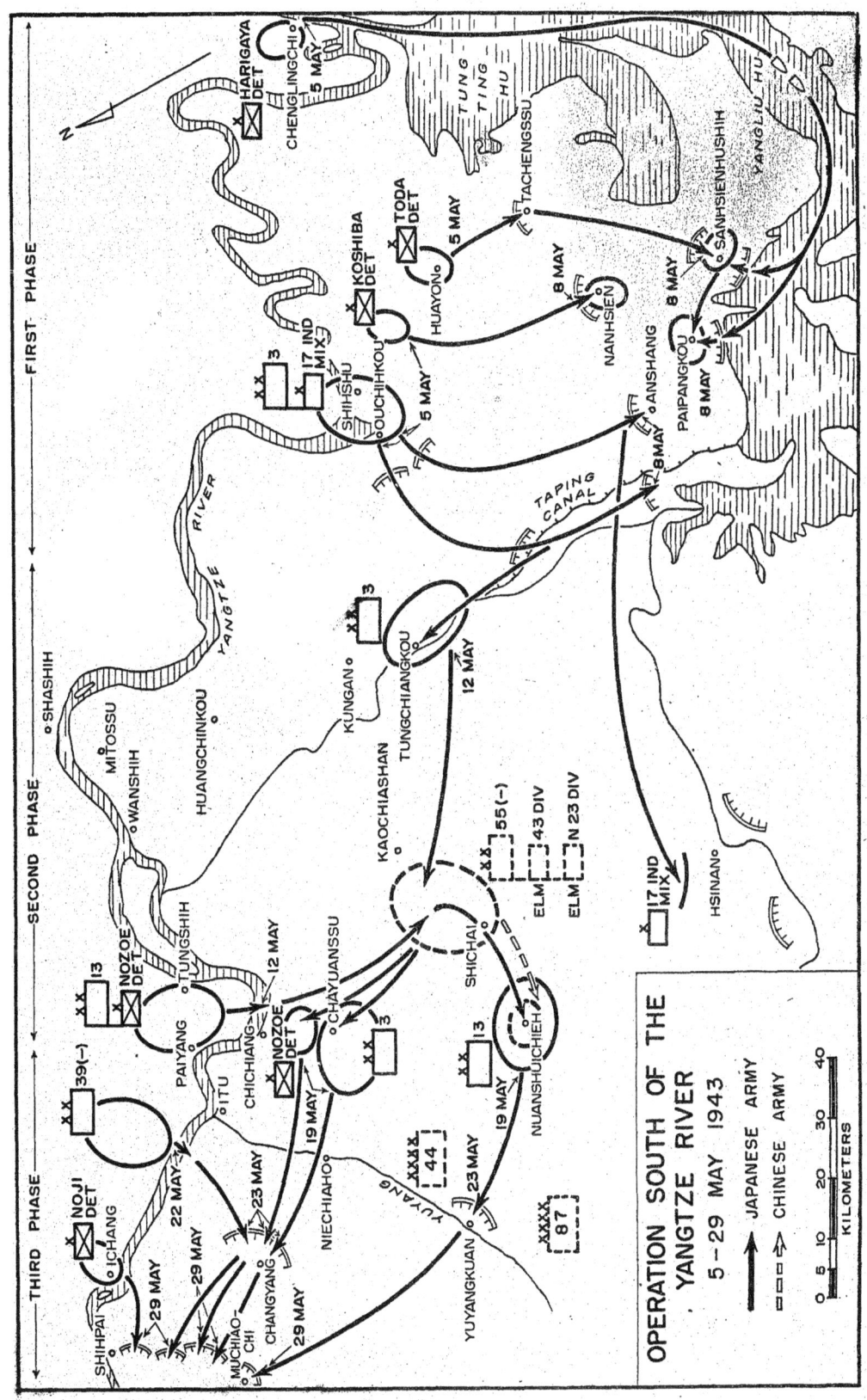

area west of Anshang and intercepted the enemy's route of retreat to the west. By the 8th, the various 11th Army groups had enveloped and destroyed the main force of the enemy south of Anshang.

The first phase of the operation terminated on 11 May.

The Koshiba, Toda and Harigaya Detachments, which had participated in this phase of the operation, remained in the occupied areas during the second phase in order to secure this region.

Second Phase:

In accordance with Army orders, the 3d Division concentrated its strength near Tungchiangkou so that it might prepare for the second phase of the operation. The 13th Division and the Nozoe Detachment concentrated their units in the area north of Chichiang and on the left bank of the Yangtze River while the 17th Independent Mixed Brigade moved westward to the sector north of Hsinan to protect the Army's rear left flank. The enemy was disposed between Chichiang and Kungan.

On 12 May, the Army opened its attack. After successfully crossing the river near Chichiang, the 13th Division advanced southward. The 3d Division initiated its offensive from Tunchiangkou toward the northwest. They attacked the enemy on both flanks simultaneously from the north and south, defeated the main force of the Chinese 55th Division, elements of the 43d Division, and the newly organized 23d Division and then captured or annihilated the fleeing enemy in the vicinity of Nuanshuichieh. The second phase of the operation terminated on 18 May.

After the conclusion of the second phase of the operation, the 13th Division concentrated near Nuanshuichieh and the 3d Division and the Nozoe Detachment near Chayuanssu where they prepared for the third phase.

Third Phase:

On 19 May the 11th Army began the third phase of the operation. It was planned to capture and destroy the enemy deployed in the sector between Ichang and Itu. On the 19th, the 13th Division left Nuanshuichieh at dawn and advanced northward, destroying the enemy en route. The 3d Division and the Nozoe Detachment opened their attacks from Chayuanssu and the area south of Chichiang respectively. At 0100 on the 22d, the 39th Division (less the Noji Detachment, composed mainly of three infantry battalions, which was stationed at Ichang) forded the Yangtze River about eight kilometers north of Itu and opened its offensive.

The Chinese 87th Army had sustained heavy casualties inflicted by the 13th Division during the second phase operation and, still in a state of confusion, did not seem able to resist. The Army therefore advanced without hindrance.

It was estimated that the enemy planned to use their 94th Army to check the 11th Army's advance at Yuyangkuan and on the right bank of the Yuyang Ho and their 87th Army in the mountains to the south of Yuyangkuan. It also appeared as though they planned to conduct a coordinated flank attack.

On 23 May, the 39th and 3d Divisions made a parallel thrust toward Changyang and advanced into this area. The 13th Division broke through the main force of the Chinese 10th Army Group near Yuyangkuan and continued to advance in a northwesterly direction. The Army then directed the Noji Detachment, which had been held at Ichang, to assume the offensive and pursue the enemy to the northwest of Changyang. Thus, the seemingly impregnable enemy positions west of Ichang, which had taken the enemy several years to construct, were penetrated by the 11th Army. On 29 May, the Army advanced to the Shihpai-Muchiaochi line, the objective of its offensive. On the 27th, it succeeded in compelling all ships at Ichang to descend to Shashih.

Withdrawal

From 31 May, the 11th Army began to withdraw. It directed the 3d and 39th Divisions to cross the Yangtze River at Ichang; the 13th Division to cross in the Itu-Chichiang area, and the 17th Independent Mixed Brigade and other detachments in the district east of Ouchihkou and Shihshu. The units began to withdraw as directed. Part of the 13th Division, however, was delayed in its concentration near Itu and, on 3 June, engaged in battle with the Chinese 79th Army. Consequently, the 11th Army deployed the 13th Division and the 17th Independent Mixed Brigade concentrated in the Kungan area and the Koshiba Detachment concentrated near Ouchihkou, to destroy this enemy force.

On 5 June, the 13th Division advanced from the Itu-Yangchi area toward Niechiaho where it defeated the 79th Army. It then concentrated its strength in the area southeast of Chichiang. On 6 June, the 17th Independent Mixed Brigade routed the Chinese 51st and 58th Divisions in the Kaochiashan area and then concentrated its strength in the area south of Kaochiashan.

Casualties sustained by the 11th Army during this operation were:

Dead	771
Wounded	2,746
Horses killed	420
Horses wounded	224

The Army ordered the 13th Division to effect a crossing of the Yangtze River at a point opposite Shashih and the 17th Independent Mixed Brigade and the Koshiba Detachment to cross from the Shihshu area. By 10 June, the units had completed fording the river without enemy opposition.

The 13th Division occupied the area around Wanshih, Mitossu and Huangchinkou opposite Shashih and the Toda Detachment occupied the Ouchihkou, Shihshu and Huayon area.[7]

Changte Operation

Situation Prior to the Operation

The Chinese 6th War Sector Army, dispersed in the fertile plains of Hunan were continuously harassing the 11th Army's western front. As Changte, where the headquarters of the 6th War Sector Army was located, was of great strategic importance, it was felt that a successful attack on this area would deal a considerable blow to the enemy.

After the outbreak of hostilities in the Pacific, the Chinese had sent expeditionary forces to the Burma area. By the summer of 1943, there were six Chinese divisions in this area as well as three armies concentrated in Yunnan and it was estimated that they would gradually reinforce the Burma area.

From the beginning of 1943 the American air force had been gradually reinforcing its strength in the interior of China, concentrating in Szechwan Province and in the area around Kweilin and Hengyang and had begun to attack the Japanese forces in the various areas.

---

7. As there were no official documents available in regard to this operation, details were written from information supplied from memory by Sentaro Azuma, a staff officer of the 11th Army at the time of the operation.

The Japanese 11th Army continued to hold the line linking Hsinyang, Ichang, Yoyang and Nanchang and, as a result of the offensive operation to the south of the Yangtze River, had captured the region along the right bank of the Yangtze River below Shashih.

Disposition of forces (both friendly and enemy) prior to the operation are shown on Map 20.

The situation in the Pacific was becoming critical. In the northern Pacific area, the Japanese occupation forces in the Aleutian Islands had been routed and the islands were lost to the enemy, while in the southeastern area, under pressure from a superior enemy the Japanese front line was compelled to retreat gradually.

In the European theater, in early August Italy sued for an armistice and the German Army was about to lose the Ukraine.

Operational Command

In consideration of the situation both in Japan and abroad, the China Expeditionary Army felt it expedient to deal a crushing blow to the enemy and submitted its plan for the Changte Operation to Imperial General Headquarters. Imperial General Headquarters recognized the necessity for increasing pressure on the enemy in this area and also for suppressing the enemy's diversion of strength to the Yunnan area but only within the limits of its plans for employing the entire strength of the Japanese armed forces.

On 27 September, Imperial General Headquarters ordered the com-

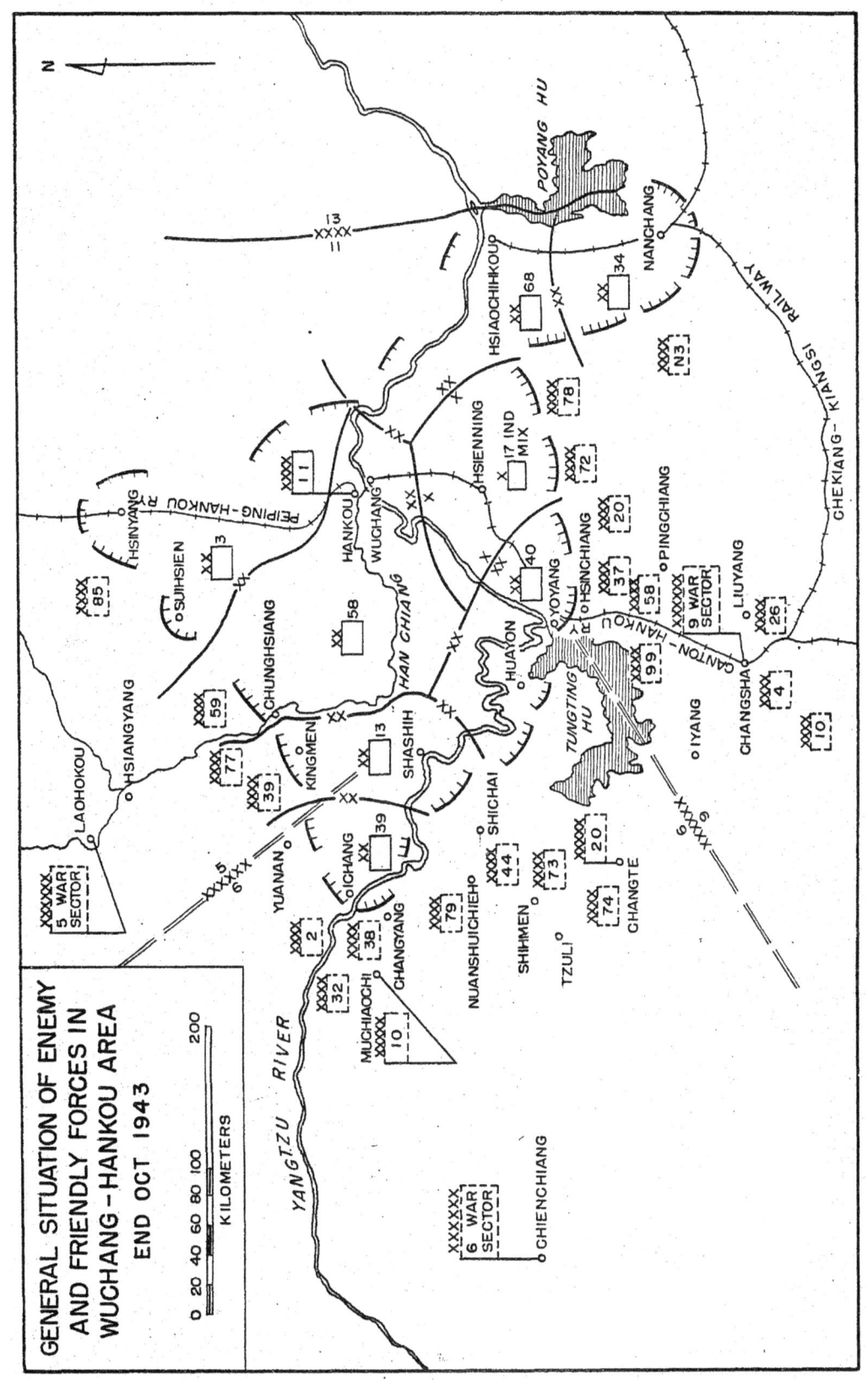

mander of the China Expeditionary Army to execute a temporary operation in the region beyond his operational area in central China in order to continue his present mission. The commander of the China Expeditionary Army, in turn, ordered the 11th Army commander to advance to the Changte area and crush the enemy's fighting strength. The order read: "The 11th Army will advance to the Changte area, attack vigorously and weaken the enemy's will to continue the war. At the same time, the Army will suppress the enemy's diversion of strength to the Burma area and will coordinate with the operation of the Southern Army."

Operational Plan

An operational plan was drawn up which stated:

> The main force of the 11th Army (approximately 35 infantry battalions, including those forces moved from other areas) will advance rapidly from the Tungshih and Shihshu areas and capture the Changte area, destroying the enemy everywhere en route.
> Successively, the enemy assembling in and counterattacking from the Changte area will be sought out and destroyed.
> After the operational objective has been attained, the Army will begin its withdrawal to its former station at an opportune time, taking into consideration the possibility of enemy counterattacks from Burma.

For this operation the China Expeditionary Army transferred to the 11th Army the Tsukabe Detachment (two infantry battalions) from the North China Area Army's 12th Army and the 116th Division from the 13th Army.

The 11th Army planned to divide the operation into three phases. During the first and second phases it planned to destroy the enemy in the area north of Changte and in Changte respectively. The withdrawal would be conducted during the third phase.

The following strength was to be employed:

    3d Division

    13th Division

    39th Division

    68th Division — Toda Detachment (three infantry battalions and one mountain artillery battalion from the 40th Division) attached.

    116th Division

    Sasaki Detachment (three infantry battalions and one mountain artillery battalion from the 34th Division)

    Miyawaki Detachment (three infantry battalions from the 17th Independent Mixed Brigade)

    Tsukabe Detachment (two infantry battalions from the 32d Division)

<u>Concentration</u>

With the prime objective the destruction of the enemy north of Changte, the 11th Army planned to dispose an element in the region southwest of Itu to protect the Army's right rear flank from the enemy to the west of Ichang while the main force would advance toward Changte, seek the enemy and attack. The plan for the concentration of the various units was to be carried out before 31 October as follows:

 3d Division - Hohsueh and the region to the northwest

 13th Division - Chiangling and the region to the southeast

 39th Division - region west of Chiangling, excluding Chiangling

 68th Division - Chienli and the region to the west

 116th Division - Region north of Shihshu

 Sasaki Detachment - To the rear of the 3d Division

 Miyawaki Detachment - To the rear of the 13th Division

 Tsukabe Detachment - This Detachment did not arrive in the combat area until after the termination of the first phase of the operation

The right bank of the Yangtze River had previously been occupied by elements of the 13th and 40th Divisions but after the completion of the concentration of the various Army groups the 13th Division unit was returned to its former command while the 40th Division unit became the Toda Detachment and was attached to the 68th Division.

After the concentration of the various units was completed on the left bank of the Yangtze River, the 11th Army ordered units deployed along the right bank of the river with all movements being conducted at night.

Lines of Communication

All the principal roads had been destroyed but, having regard to previous experience, it was felt that it would not be feasible to attempt to repair the roads. As the operational zone was a rice-producing area, supplies could be obtained locally and it was planned to supply aummunition only at the Li Shui line and at Changte.

Progress of Operation

As the concentration of its forces had progressed as planned, on 28 October the 11th Army decided to have its main force destroy the Chinese 79th Army in the Wangchiachang area while an element was to destroy the enemy 44th Army near Anshang. The offensive was to be initiated at dusk on 2 November, the confronting enemy destroyed and the units to advance to the following points:

    39th Division - to the region southwest of Itu

    13th Division - to the Nuanshuichieh area

    Miyawaki Detachment - to the Nuanshuichieh area (following the 13th Division)

    3d Division - to the region southwest of Wangchiachang

Sasaki Detachment — to the Wangchiachang area, following the 3d Division

116th Division — to the Anshang area

68th Division (Toda Detachment attached) — to the Anshang area

The Tsukabe Detachment, which arrived in the combat area at the end of the first phase was ordered to advance to Hsinan in order to protect the Army's right rear flank.

By night of 30 October, the first-line troops had advanced to the south bank of the Yangtze River. By 1 November, deployment of the forces was completed and at dusk on 2 November the offensive began. After routing small bands of enemy troops on the way, on 5 November the 13th and 3d Divisions attacked the enemy at the Nuanshuichieh-Wangchiachang line while the 116th and 68th Divisions attacked the 44th Army near Anshang. The 13th and 3d Divisions continued to pursue the enemy on 5 and 6 November and, on the 9th, advanced to Miaoling and Hsinmenssu respectively. About this time, the Miyawaki Detachment advanced to Nuanshuichieh and the Sasaki Detachment to Hsinkuan. The 116th and 68th Divisions attacked both flanks of the enemy massed near Anshang and the enemy immediately began to withdraw. The 116th Division then moved to the area north of Chingshih and attacked an element of the 44th Army entrenched there. The Chinese troops retreated to the southwest without making any noticeable resistance. In order to destroy the Chinese 73d Army in the vicinity of Shihmen the 11th Army then ordered the 3d Division and the Sasaki Detachment to attack both flanks of this Army, the 116th Division to advance toward Chichiaho, the 68th Division to advance by water toward the southwest of Hanshou and the Miyawaki Detachment (disposed at Nuanshuichieh) and the Koga Detachment (disposed between the Miyawaki Detachment and the 13th Division) to protect the Army's rear right flank. (Map 21)

Between 14 and 16 November, the 3d Division and the Sasaki Detachment attacked and defeated the Chinese 73d Army.

The first phase of the operation terminated on 16 November.

The 11th Army's objective during the second phase of the operation was to destroy the enemy in the proximity of Changte and to capture the town. It ordered the 13th Division (with the Sasaki Detachment attached) together with the 3d and 116th Divisions to attack the Chinese 74th, 44th and other armies to the south of Tzuli and in the vicinity of Chichiaho while the 68th Division was ordered to attack the enemy at Hanshou.

The Japanese army groups commenced their actions on 19 November and by 21 November had defeated the 74th Army near Chichiaho. Subsequently, the 3d and 116th Divisions advanced toward the area south of Changte by way of Taoyuan and to Changte by way of Tsuishih respectively. The 13th Division, however, met stubborn resistance from an enemy which took full advantage of the mountainous terrain.

MAP NO. 21

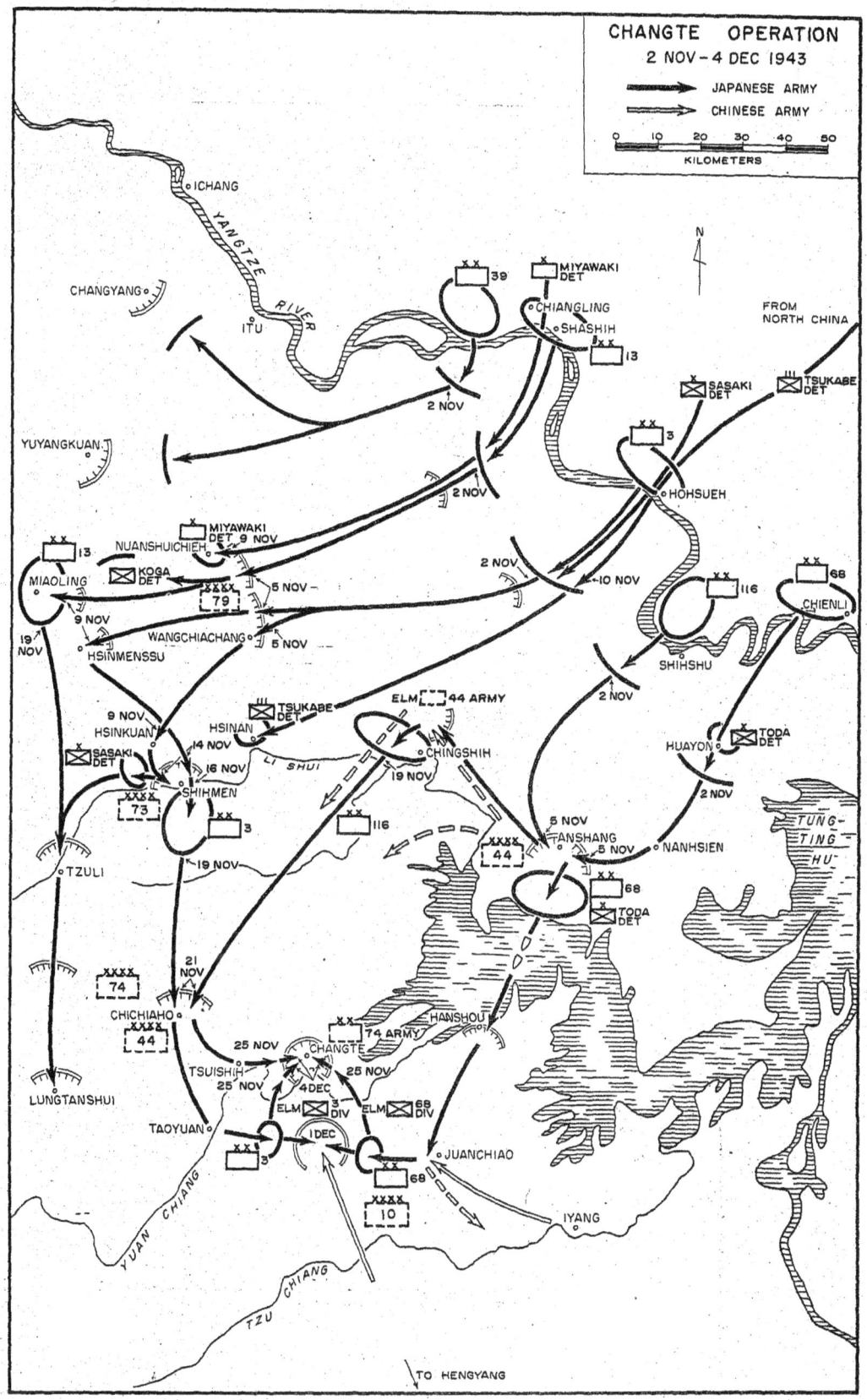

After capturing Hanshou, the 68th Division annihilated the enemy around Iyang in the neighborhood of Juanchiao and advanced to the area south of Changte where, together with the 3d Division, it was ordered to destroy enemy reinforcements arriving from the south.

On 23 November, the 11th Army ordered the main force of the 116th Division together with elements of the 68th and 3d Divisions, to capture Changte. On the 25th, this force opened its attack but one division of the 74th Army, which was occupying Changte, resisted stubbornly. During this time, the Chinese 10th Army advanced north from Hengyang to reinforce Changte, crossed the Tzu Chiang and attacked the Japanese forces. As the enemy had advanced through the area between the 3d and 68th Divisions, the divisions effected a pincer movement and, on 1 December, destroyed this force.

In spite of continued resistance on the part of the enemy, on 4 December, the 11th Army occupied Changte.

The Army then adjusted its positions on the northern bank of the Yuan Chiang and was on the verge of withdrawing when an inquiry was received from Imperial General Headquarters, through the Commander in Chief of the China Expeditionary Army, concerning the possibility of maintaining Changte in preparation for the Ichigo

Operation[8] which was to be conducted the following year. The Army objected on the grounds that it was impossible to alter the present operational plan and, on 9 December, ordered the various units to withdraw to the Li Shui starting on the night of the 11th. By the 13th, the Army groups had completed their withdrawal to the right bank of the Li Shui without interference from the enemy. However, the China Expeditionary Army ordered the 11th Army to halt at this line. Withdrawals were suspended but, after prolonged and intricate negotiations with Imperial General Headquarters, the 11th Army was permitted to return to its former positions. On the night 19 December, the withdrawals were again begun and, by 24 December, the 11th Army had returned to its original positions.[9]

Japanese casualties during this operation were 1,274 dead and 2,977 wounded.

---

8. See Monograph No 72, **Army Operations in China, Jan 44-Aug 45**.

9. No official records of this operation exist; therefore, details given above were constructed from the memoirs of Colonel Seitaro Takei, a staff officer of the 11th Army at the time of the operation.

INDEX

Air Brigade
  1st: 19-20, 31, 54, 57, 64, 72, 80, 87, 90
Air Division
  3d: 20
Air Regiment
  16th: 21
  44th: 19, 21, 72, 143-44, 150
  45th: 19, 31
  54th: 19, 21
  62d: 91
  90th: 21, 91
Air Squadron
  Independent
    10th: 19, 21
    18th: 19, 21
    83d: 19, 21
Air Unit
  Direct Cooperation
    8th: 19, 21
Ani: 72
Anshang: 149-50, 153, 164-65
Army
  1st: 16, 19-20, 126-27
  11th: 19-20, 53-54, 62, 64-66, 71-73, 80, 85, 87-91, 99-00, 103-04, 111-12, 115-16, 121, 126-27, 138-40, 150, 153, 154-58, 161-62, 164, 166, 169-70
  12th: 19, 20, 161
  13th: 17, 19-20, 66, 79-80, 85, 87, 89-92, 96, 103-06, 109-10, 116-17, 121, 127, 137, 156, 161
  23d: 16, 18-19, 22, 27-28, 30-31, 32-33, 37-38, 48, 53-54, 75, 91, 126-27, 130
  China Expeditionary: 18, 20, 27, 31, 37, 49, 54, 79, 85-87, 98, 103, 105, 116, 117, 121, 123-25, 129, 137, 148, 158, 161, 169-70
  Kwantung: 105
  Mongolian Garrison: 19
  North China Area: 18, 85, 88, 90, 105, 127, 161
  Southern: 18, 20, 37, 54, 91, 161
Battalion
  Independent Antitank Gun
    2d: 46
    5th: 46
Brigade
  Harada Mixed: 87, 97, 106, 110, 118
  Independent Mixed
    1st: 18
    2d: 19
    3d: 19
    4th: 19, 127
    5th: 19
    6th: 19, 127
    7th: 18
    8th: 18
    9th: 19, 54, 57-58, 63, 66, 69, 71
    10th: 19
    11th: 19
    12th: 19, 127
    13th: 19, 127
    14th: 19, 54, 57, 72-73
    15th: 18, 127
    16th: 19
    17th: 19, 141, 149-50, 153, 155-56, 162
    18th: 19, 54, 57, 74
    19th: 19, 22, 27
    20th: 19
    22d: 127
    23d: 127, 130, 133
  Kono Mixed: 88, 89-90, 95-98, 106, 117-18
  Kozonoe Mixed: 88, 96-98, 109, 117-18
Burma: 53, 126, 157, 161
Canton: 18, 22, 38, 48, 53, 63, 131
Changan: 123
Changchiachi: 74
Changhsing: 137
Changlochen: 91-92
Changlochieh: 58, 64, 66, 71
Changsha: 63-64, 66, 72, 112, 143

Changshuchen: 115
Changsing: 79, 89
Changte: 157, 161-64, 166, 169
Changyang: 155
Chanpinghsu: 100, 103
Chayuanssu: 154
Chekiang-Kiangsi: 111
Chen Cheng: 75
Chenghsien: 91, 117
Chenglingchi: 149
Chengtu: 123
Chengyuehshih: 133
Chiang
    Chientan: 17, 89
    Chin: 73
    Chu: 118
    Fuchun: 92, 95, 97, 99, 106, 117
    Ou: 110
    Tzu: 169
    Yuan: 169
Chiang Kai-shek: 15
Chiangling: 163
Chiangshan: 106
Chiaotung: 115
Chichiaho: 166
Chichiang: 149, 153-55
Chienchiapo: 75
Chienli: 143, 163
Chiente: 92
Chinchi: 104
Chinching: 64-66
Chinese Army
    3d: 72-73, 87
    4th: 48, 63, 63n, 112
    9th: 92
    10th: 63-64, 169
    20th: 58, 63n, 69
    26th: 63n, 80n, 97
    35th: 116
    37th: 62-65
    44th: 164-66
    58th: 63n, 69, 111-12, 115
    73th: 63n, 70, 166
    74th: 48, 63n, 80n, 97, 166, 169
    78th: 63n, 69
    79th: 63n, 100, 103-04, 111, 156, 164
    87th: 154-55
    94th: 154
    99th: 61-62, 63n, 69-70
    100th: 100, 104
    Communist: 141
    Nationalist: 79, 141
    War Sector
        3d: 80, 86-87, 91, 96-97, 100
        4th: 22, 48
        5th: 73, 80
        6th: 63n, 73, 80, 157
        9th: 48, 61, 63, 80, 100, 111
Chinese Army Group
    10th: 155
    23d: 79, 89
    30th: 62, 73
    32d: 79, 89
Chinese Division
    7th Cavalry: 16
    23th: 153
    27th: 75
    43d: 153
    51st: 156
    55th: 153
    58th: 156
    95th: 65
    128th: 90
    132d: 74
    179th: 74
Chinese Group
    Garrison 4th: 133
Chingshih: 165
Chinhsien: 100
Chinhua: 86-87, 91-92, 95-97, 106, 110, 116-18
Chin I-wu: 144
Chiuchiang: 22
Chuangshuchiao: 63
Chuchi: 86, 91
Chuchou: 63
Chuhoshih: 143
Chuhsien: 86, 91, 95-98, 103, 106, 111, 117-18

Chunghsiang: 74
Chungjen: 103, 112, 115
Chungking: 53, 122-23, 130
Chunhuashan: 66, 69
Company
  Bridging Material
    1st: 46
    2d: 46
Detachments
  Araki: 22, 33, 34, 38, 48
  Harigaya: 149-50, 153
  Hirano: 89, 111
  Ide: 88, 99-100, 103-04, 111, 115
  Imai: 88, 99-100, 103-04, 111-12, 115
  Iwanaga: 99-100, 104
  Koga: 166
  Koshiba: 149-50, 153, 156
  Miyawaki: 162-66
  Nara: 105, 109-10
  Noguchi: 57-58
  Noji: 154-55
  Nozoe: 149, 153-54
  Sasaki: 162-63, 165-66
  Sawa: 57, 61, 63, 65, 71
  Takehara: 88, 100, 103-04, 111-12, 115-16
  Toda: 149-50, 153, 156, 162-63
  Tozono: 57-58, 66, 69, 71
  Tsukabe: 162-63, 165
  Yazu: 99, 104
Division
  3d: 19, 54, 58, 61, 62, 64, 69, 70, 72, 75, 88, 99-100, 103-04, 111-12, 115, 141, 149-50, 153-55, 162-66, 169
  4th: 16, 20, 53-54
  5th: 16, 20
  6th: 19, 54, 57-58, 61-62, 64, 69-71, 88, 90, 126, 141
  13th: 19, 75, 142-44, 147, 149, 153-56, 162-66
  15th: 19, 87, 89, 92, 95-98, 106, 117-18, 126
  17th: 19, 87, 126
  18th: 16, 20, 22
  21st: 16, 20
  22th: 19, 87, 89, 92, 95-98, 106, 111, 117-18
  26th: 19, 88
  27th: 18
  32d: 19, 88, 91-92, 95, 97-98, 106, 118, 162
  33d: 16, 20
  34th: 19, 54, 57, 72, 88, 99-100, 103-04, 111, 149, 162
  35th: 18
  36th: 19, 126
  37th: 19
  38th: 16, 20, 22, 27, 29-30, 32, 35, 37-38, 47
  39th: 19, 53, 74, 149, 154-55, 162-64
  40th: 19, 54, 57-58, 61-62, 64-66, 69-70, 88, 142-44, 147, 149, 162-63
  41st: 19, 126
  48th: 22, 27
  51st: 19-20, 22, 35, 126
  58th: 20, 142-44, 147, 149, 156
  59th: 20
  60th: 20, 137-38
  61st: 127, 137-38
  62d: 127
  63d: 127
  64th: 127
  65th: 127
  68th: 20, 88-89, 162-63, 165-66, 169
  69th: 20
  70th: 20, 87, 92, 95-96, 98, 106, 109, 111, 117-18, 137
  104th: 19, 22, 32
  110th: 17-18
  116th: 19, 87, 89, 92, 95, 97-98, 106, 111, 118, 161-63, 165-66, 169
Fenchiachiao: 71-72
Fenghua: 91, 117
Fengkow: 143-44

Fleet
   China Area: 89, 130
   China Expeditionary 2d: 31, 130
Fuchang: 144
Fulinpu: 66, 69-71
Fuyang: 86
Haikang: 133
Hakwaichung: 21
Hangchou: 86-87, 90, 105, 117
Hankou: 90
Hanshou: 166, 169
Hengfeng: 99, 104
Hengyang: 157, 169
Hill
   Braemar: 45-46
   Cove: 36
   Golden: 37
   Grassy: 36
   Hebe: 21
   Violet: 47
Ho
   Fu: 100, 111-12, 116
   Hsin: 111, 116
   Hsinchiang: 58, 71
   Huang: 17
   Kan: 99-100
   Laotao: 63n, 70
   Liuyang: 63n, 64, 66, 69
   Shachiang: 58
   Yuyang: 155
Hohsueh: 163
Hong Kong: 15-18, 20-22, 27-32, 35-37, 42, 45-49, 53, 63, 75-76, 130n, 133
Hsiangtung: 74
Hsiaochihkou: 138
Hsiaoshunchen: 95
Hsiehfoushih: 99
Hsinan: 153, 165
Hsinchang: 117
Hsinchiang: 58
Hsinkaishih: 62, 66, 69, 71
Hsinkuan: 165
Hsinlaitsun: 133
Hsinmenssu: 165

Hsinshih: 61-62, 69, 71
Hsinyang: 138, 158
Hsishanwanshoukung: 72
Hsitang: 58
Hsiushui: 62
Hsiutsaifou: 103, 112, 115
Hsuancheng: 79, 89, 134, 137
Hu
   Hung: 144
   Kucheng: 137
   Pailu: 143-44
   Poyang: 80, 89
   Sha: 143
   Tai: 137
   Tanani: 137
   Tungting: 142, 147, 150
   Yangliu: 150
Huamenlou: 65
Huangchiachi: 74
Huangchinkou: 156
Huayon: 149-50, 157
Hukou: 80
Humen: 28, 30, 35, 38
Ichang: 75, 123, 129, 138, 148-49, 154-55, 158, 162
Ihuang: 112
Imperial General Headquarters: 16, 20, 27, 31, 37, 48, 53, 79, 85-87, 90, 99, 105, 116, 121-22, 124, 129-30, 158, 169
Island
   Aleutian: 158
   Hainan: 22, 27, 133
   Stonecutter: 28, 41
   Tsingi: 28, 34, 41-42
Itu: 154-55, 162, 164
Iwu: 91-92, 118
Iyang: 169
Jochi: 73
Juanchiao: 169
Jubilee Reservoir: 21, 28, 34, 37, 41-42
Kaitak: 41-42
Kaoan: 72-73
Kaochiashan: 156
Kaupingfong: 36

Kengkou: 58
Kenji Shindo, Lt Col: 138n
Kingmen: 74
Korechika Anami, Lt Gen: 54, 76n
Kowloon: 30, 34, 37, 42, 45
Kuan Chuan: 74
Kuangchou Wan: 129-30
Kuangfeng: 98, 106
Kuangte: 79, 85, 89, 134, 137
Kuangyuan: 123
Kuanwangchiao: 58, 61, 63
Kuanyinssu: 74
Kueichi: 104, 111, 116
Kueichih: 17
Kueii: 61-62
Kungan: 149, 153, 156
Kungtongtsai: 45
Kweilin: 157
Laichiatsi: 74
Lanchi: 86, 91-92, 95-96, 106, 117-18
Langchi: 17
Langlishih: 64, 66, 69-70
Lanshihho: 71-72
Lichi: 112
Lichiachung: 64, 70
Lichiao: 69-70
Linchuan: 100, 103-04, 111-12
Lishui: 86, 96, 98, 109, 111, 117
Liuyang: 112
Liyang: 137
Lochiahsiang: 58
Luchiao: 61
Lungyu: 95-97, 106, 110
Mafengtsui: 64
Malay: 28
Malinshih: 66, 69
Manchuria: 124
Miaoling: 165
Mienyang: 138, 143-44
Mitossu: 156
Mountain
    Maonshan: 28, 34, 37
    Mashihshan: 62, 70
    Nicholson: 47

Pakshakiu: 36
Piaofengshan: 70
    Taimaoshan: 28, 34, 36, 41
    Tamoshan: 62, 64, 70
    Taohuashan: 62
    Tapashan: 65, 69
    Tapiehshan: 141
    Yingchushan: 71
Muchiaochi: 155
Nanchang: 62, 72, 99, 121, 138, 158
Nancheng: 99, 103-04, 111, 115-16
Nanching: 17, 134, 137
Nanhai: 22, 38
Nanhsien: 149-50
Nanling: 137
Niechiaho: 156
Ningpo: 117
Nuanshuichieh: 154, 164-66
Operation
    1st Changsha: 76
    2d Changsha: 17, 53, 66, 72, 75-76, 80n
    3d Changsha: 17n
    Changte: 157-58
    Chekiang-Kiangsi: 79, 80n, 90-91, 99, 141
    Hong Kong: 17, 21, 27, 30-31, 32-33, 48, 53
    Ichigo: 169
    Kuangte: 134, 137
    Lishui: 97-98
    Luichow Peninsula: 129
    Malay: 16
    Mienyang: 90
    Seigo-Kosaku: 137
    Southern Invasion: 20
    Sungyang: 109-10
    Szechwan: 124
    Wuchang-Hankou: 134
    Yungchia: 109
Ouchihkou: 150, 155-57
Paimachai: 103, 115
Paipangkou: 150
Paipo: 115
Paitouchen: 91

Paiyang: 149
Panmaotien: 65
Paoan: 35-36, 38
Pawangcheng: 17
Peichiatsun: 133
Peninsula
   Kowloon: 21, 27-28, 35-37, 42
   Luichow: 129-30, 134
   Taitam: 46
Pingchiang: 62, 73
Pinghai: 34
Pi Yueh: 61, 111
Province
   Anhwei: 138
   Chekiang: 79, 85-87, 90, 110, 116
   Honan: 17
   Hopeh: 15, 17-18
   Hunan: 157
   Kiangsi: 100, 141
   Kiangsu: 138
   Kwangsi: 48, 53, 63n
   Kwangtung: 63n, 80n
   Shansi: 15-16, 18, 123
   Shantung: 15, 17-18
   Suiyuan: 15-16
   Szechwan: 121-23, 157
   Yunnan: 53, 157-58
Putang: 65
Railway
   Canton-Hankou: 61
   Canton-Kowloon: 22, 35
   Chekiang-Kiangsi: 96, 99, 100, 104-06, 111, 116
   Nanchang-Hsiaochihkou: 54
Regiment
   Engineer
      38th: 46
   Independent Engineer
      14th: 46
      20th: 46
   Infantry
      228th: 42, 46
      229th: 36-38, 42, 46
      230th: 38, 46
   Independent Mountain Artillery
      10th: 46
      20th: 46
   Mountain Artillery
      38th: 46
Sanchiangkou: 61, 63, 100, 103-04, 111
Sanhsienhushih: 150
Sano Group (same to the 38th Div): 41
Sanshui: 22, 38
Sauki Wan: 45-46
Sautu: 73
Seitaro Takei, Colonel: 170
Sentaro Azuma, Major: 147n, 157n
Shafoutan: 99
Shanchiahsu: 73
Shanghai: 16, 20, 53
Shangjao: 86, 98-99, 103, 106
Shanwei: 22, 27, 34, 38
Shaohsing: 86
Shashih: 143, 148, 155, 158
Shatau: 36
Shataukok: 36
Shenchuanhsu: 22, 28, 30, 35-36, 38
Sheungshui: 22
Shiangpichiao: 70
Shihlung: 28, 30
Shihmen: 166
Shihmenshih: 117
Shihpai: 155
Shihshu: 148-49, 155-57, 161, 163
Shouchang: 95
Shui
   Fengcheng: 115
   Ihuang: 103, 112, 115
   Ku: 61-63, 71
   Li: 164, 170
Solomon: 124
Su Chen-Tung: 147
Suichang: 110
Suichi: 133
Suihsien: 75
Sungyang: 109
Swatou: 22
Tachengssu: 150

Tachingchieh: 58
Taifou: 137
Taipo: 36, 41
Taiwai: 34
Taiwantsun: 45
Takashi Sakai, Lt Gen: 22
Tangchi: 95
Taniangchiao: 62
Tanshui: 22, 27, 34, 38, 48
Taoyuan: 166
Taping Canal: 150
Tate's Cairn: 21, 37, 42
Tengchiafou: 104
Tichiang: 79, 89
Tide Cove: 34, 41, 42
Tsenglanshu: 42
Tsengtsun: 115
Tsuishih: 166
Tsunghua: 91
Tuchang: 111
Tuchiawei: 103
Tungchiangkou: 153
Tunghsiang: 100, 116
Tungkuan: 38
Tungkung: 74
Tungshih: 149, 161
Tungyang: 96
Tzuli: 166
Ukraine: 158
Unit
  Field Transport 11th: 57
  Light Transport Mortar 21st: 46
  Kitajima (1st Arty): 32, 35, 38, 41
  Kitazawa: 32
  Kobayashi: 33
  Sato: 33

Wanchihchen: 89, 134, 137
Wangchiachang: 164-65
Wang Chin-Tsai: 141, 144
Wang Government: 126n
Wanhsien: 123
Wanshechien: 99
Wanshin: 156
Wengchiang: 62
Wuchang-Hankou: 15, 17, 54, 80, 134, 138, 147
Wuhu: 89
Wui: 95-96, 98, 117-18
Wukang: 137
Wukungshih: 69
Wushihchien: 64
Wuwan: 111-12, 116
Yangchi: 156
Yangping: 75
Yangtze River: 15, 17, 54, 73, 80, 89, 134, 136, 138-42, 147-48, 153-54, 156, 158, 163-65
Yankamtau: 36
Yinchihsu: 100
Yintanchen: 103-04
Yoyang: 58, 61, 63, 66, 69, 90, 138, 143, 148, 158
Yuanan: 75
Yuantanhsu: 91
Yuehkoushih: 147
Yuenlongkauhsi: 36, 41
Yuhan Dou: 80
Yuhang: 90
Yu Hsueh-Chung: 17
Yunganshih: 66
Yungchia: 89, 109, 110, 117
Yungkang: 96, 98
Yunshanshih: 100
Yushan: 86, 98-99, 106, 110-11
Yuyangkuan: 154-55

www.ingramcontent.com/pod-product-compliance
Lightning Source LLC
Chambersburg PA
CBHW050501110426
42742CB00018B/3327